Communication:

Enhancing Your Relationships

A four-week course to help adults communicate effectively.

by
Deena Borchers

Apply-It-To-Life™
Adult
BIBLE CURRICULUM
from Group

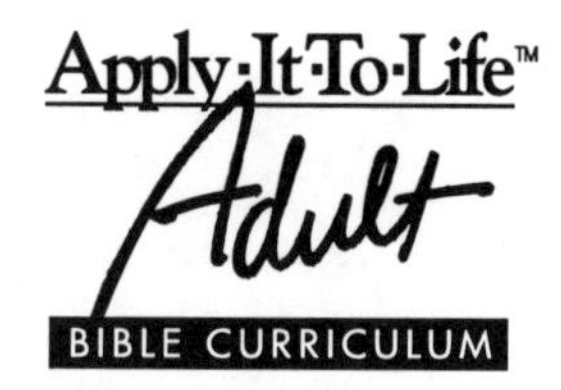

Group®

Communication: Enhancing Your Relationships

This curriculum book is a significantly revised edition of a book by the same title, copyright © 1993 Group Publishing, Inc., Box 481, Loveland, CO 80539.

Credits
Editors: Stephen Parolini and Bob Buller
Senior Editor: Paul Woods
Creative Products Director: Joani Schultz
Interior Designer: Kathy Benson
Cover Designer: Liz Howe
Cover Photographer: Daniel Allan; FPG International
Illustrator: Amy Bryant

ISBN 1-55945-512-8

10 9 8 7 6 5 4 3 2 1 04 03 02 01 00 99 98 97 96 95

Printed in the United States of America.

C O N T E N T S

Introduction

What Is Apply-It-To-Life™ Adult Bible Curriculum?

Apply-It-To-Life™ Adult Bible Curriculum is a series of four-week study courses designed to help you facilitate powerful lessons that will help adults grow in faith. Use this course with

- Sunday school classes,
- home study groups,
- weekday Bible study groups,
- men's Bible studies,
- women's Bible studies, and
- family classes.

The variety of courses gives the adult student a broad coverage of topical, life-related issues and significant biblical topics. In addition, as the name of the series implies, every lesson helps the adult student apply Scripture to his or her life.

Each course in Apply-It-To-Life Adult Bible Curriculum provides four lessons on different aspects of one topic. In each course, you also receive Fellowship and Outreach Specials connected to the month's topic. They provide suggestions for building closer relationships in your class, outreach activities, and even a party idea!

What Makes Apply-It-To-Life Adult Bible Curriculum Unique?

Teaching as Jesus Taught

Jesus was a master teacher. With Apply-It-To-Life Adult Bible Curriculum, you'll use the same teaching methods and principles that Jesus used:

- **Active Learning.** Think back on an important lesson you've learned in life. Did you learn it from reading about it? from hearing about it? from something you did? Chances are, the most important lessons you've learned came from something you experienced. That's what active learning is—learning by doing. Active learning leads students through activities and experiences that help them understand important principles, messages, and ideas. It's a discovery process that helps people internalize and remember what they learn.

Jesus often used active learning. One of the most vivid examples is his washing of his disciples' feet. In Apply-It-To-Life Adult Bible Curriculum, the teacher might remove his or her shoes and socks then read aloud the foot-washing passage from John 13, or the teacher might choose to actually wash people's feet. Participants won't soon forget it. Active learning uses simple activities to teach profound lessons.

● **Interactive Learning.** Interactive learning means learning through small-group interaction and discussion. While it may seem to be a simple concept, it's radically new to many churches that have stuck with a lecture format or large-group discussion for so long. With interactive learning, each person is actively involved in discovering God's truth through talking with other people about God's Word. Interactive learning is discussion with a difference. It puts people in pairs, trios, or foursomes to involve everyone in the learning experience. It takes active learning a step further by having people who have gone through an experience teach others what they've learned.

Jesus often helped cement the learning from an experience by questioning people—sometimes in small groups—about what had happened. He regularly questioned his followers and his opponents, forcing them to think and to discuss among themselves what he was teaching them. After washing his disciples' feet, the first thing Jesus did was ask the disciples if they understood what he had done. After the "foot washing" activity, the teacher might form small groups and have people discuss how they felt when the leader removed his or her shoes and socks. Then group members could compare those feelings and the learning involved to what the disciples must have experienced.

● **Biblical Depth.** Apply-It-To-Life Adult Bible Curriculum recognizes that most adults are ready to go below the surface to better understand the deeper truths of the Bible. Therefore, the activities and studies go beyond an "easy answer" approach to Christian education and lead adults to grapple with difficult issues from a biblical perspective.

Each lesson begins by giving the teacher resource material on the Bible passages covered in the study. In the Bible Basis, you'll find information that will help you understand the Scriptures you're dealing with. Within the class-time section of the lesson, thought-provoking activities and discussions lead adults to new depths of biblical understanding. Bible Insights within the lesson give pertinent information that will bring the Bible to life for you and your class members. In-class handouts give adults significant Bible information and challenge them to search for and discover biblical truths for themselves. Finally, the "For Even Deeper Discussion" sections provide questions that will lead your class members to new and deeper levels of insight and application.

No one questions the depth of Jesus' teachings or the effectiveness of his teaching methods. This curriculum follows Jesus' example and helps people probe the depths of the Bible in a way no other adult curriculum does.

- **Bible Application.** Jesus didn't stop with helping people understand truth. For him, teaching took the learner beyond understanding to application. It wasn't enough that the rich young ruler knew all the right answers. Jesus wanted him to take action on what he knew. In the same way, Apply-It-To-Life Adult Bible Curriculum encourages a response in people's lives. That's why this curriculum is called "Apply-It-To-Life"! Depth of understanding means little if the truths of Scripture don't zing into people's hearts. Each lesson brings home one point and encourages people to consider the changes they might make in response.
- **One Purpose.** In each study, every activity works toward communicating and applying the same point. People may discover other new truths, but the study doesn't load them down with a mass of information. Sometimes less is more. When lessons try to teach too much, they often fail to teach anything. Even Jesus limited his teaching to what he felt people could really learn and apply (John 16:12). Apply-It-To-Life Adult Bible Curriculum makes sure that class members thoroughly understand and apply one point each week.
- **Variety.** People appreciate variety. Jesus constantly varied his teaching methods. One day he would have a serious discussion with his disciples about who he was and another day he'd baffle them by turning water into wine. What he didn't do was allow them to become bored with what he had to teach them.

Any kind of study can become less than exciting if the leader and students do everything the same way week after week. Apply-It-To-Life Adult Bible Curriculum varies activities and approaches to keep everyone's interest level high each week. In one class, you might have people in small groups "put themselves in the disciples' sandals" and experience something of the confusion of Jesus' death and resurrection. In another lesson, class members may experience problems in communication and examine how such problems can damage relationships.

To meet adults' varied needs, the courses cover a wide range of topics such as Jesus, knowing God's will, communication, taking faith to work, and highlights of Bible books. One month you may choose to study a family or personal faith issue; the next month you may cover a biblical topic such as the book of John.

- **Relevance.** People today want to know how to live successfully right now. They struggle with living as authentic Christians at work, in the family, and in the community. Most churchgoing adults want to learn about the Bible, but not merely for the sake of having greater Bible knowledge. They want to know how the Bible can help them live faithful lives—how it can help them face the difficulties of living in today's culture. Apply-It-To-Life Adult Bible Curriculum bridges the gap between biblical truth and the "real world" issues of people's lives. Jesus didn't discuss with his followers the eschatological significance of Ezekiel's wheels, and Apply-It-To-Life Adult Bible Curriculum won't either! Courses and studies in this curriculum focus on the real needs of people and help them discover answers in Scripture that will help meet those needs.
- **A Nonthreatening Atmosphere.** In many adult classes, people feel intimidated because they're new Christians or because they don't have the Bible knowledge they think they should have. Jesus sometimes intimidated those who opposed him, but he consistently treated his followers with understanding and respect. We want people in church to experience the same understanding and respect Jesus' followers experienced. With Apply-It-To-Life Adult Bible Curriculum, no one is embarrassed for not knowing or understanding as much as someone else. In fact, the interactive learning process minimizes the differences between those with vast Bible knowledge and those with little Bible knowledge. Lessons often begin with nonthreatening, sharing questions and move slowly toward more depth. Whatever their level of knowledge or commitment, class members will work together to discover biblical truths that can affect their lives.
- **A Group That Cares.** Jesus began his ministry by choosing a group of 12 people who learned from him together. That group practically lived together—sharing one another's hurts, joys, and ambitions. Sometimes Jesus divided the 12 into smaller groups and worked with just three or four at a time.

Studies have shown that many adults today long for a close-knit group of people with whom they can share personal needs and joys. And people interact more freely when they feel accepted in a group. Activities in this curriculum will help class members get to know one another better and care for one another more as they study the Bible and apply its truths to their lives. As people reveal their thoughts and feelings to one another, they'll grow closer and develop more commitment to the group and to each other. And they'll be encouraging one another along the way!

● **An Element of Delight.** We don't often think about Jesus' ministry in this way, but there certainly were times he brought fun and delight to his followers. Remember the time he raised Peter's mother-in-law? or the time he sat happily with children on his lap? How about the joy and excitement at his triumphal entry into Jerusalem? or the time he helped fishing disciples catch a boatload of fish—after they'd fished all night with no success?

People learn more when they're having fun. So within Apply-It-To-Life Adult Bible Curriculum, elements of fun and delight pop up often. And sometimes adding fun is as simple as using a carrot for a pretend microphone!

Taking the Fear out of Teaching

Teachers love Apply-It-To-Life Adult Bible Curriculum because it makes teaching much less stressful. Lessons in this curriculum

● **are easy to teach.** Interactive learning frees the teacher from being a dispenser of information to serve as a facilitator of learning. Teachers can spend class time guiding people to discover and apply biblical truths. The studies provide clear, understandable Bible background; easy-to-prepare learning experiences; and powerful, thought-provoking discussion questions.

● **can be prepared quickly.** Lessons in Apply-It-To-Life Adult Bible Curriculum are logical and clear. There's no sorting through tons of information to figure out the lesson. In 30 minutes, a busy teacher can easily read a lesson and prepare to teach it. In addition, optional and For Extra Time activities allow the teacher to tailor the lesson to the class. And the thorough instructions and questions will guide even an inexperienced teacher through each powerful lesson.

● **let everyone share in the class's success.** With Apply-It-To-Life Adult Bible Curriculum, the teacher is one of the participants. The teacher still guides the class, but the burden is not as heavy. Everyone participates and adds to the study's effectiveness. So when the study has an impact, everyone shares in that success.

● **lead the teacher to new discoveries.** Each lesson is designed to help the teacher first discover a biblical truth. And most teachers will make additional discoveries as they prepare each lesson. In class, the teacher will discover even more as other adults share what they have found. As with any type of teaching, the teacher will likely learn more than anyone else in the class!

● **provide relevant information to class members.** Photocopiable handouts are designed to help people better understand or interpret Bible passages. And the handouts make teaching easier because the teacher can often refer to them for small-group discussion questions and instructions.

How to Use Apply-It-To-Life Adult Bible Curriculum

First familiarize yourself with an Apply-It-To-Life Adult Bible Curriculum lesson. The following explanations will help you understand how the lesson elements work together.

Lesson Elements

● The **Opening** maps out the lesson's agenda and introduces your class to the topic for the session. Sometimes this activity will help people get better acquainted as they begin to explore the topic together.

● The **Bible Exploration and Application** activities will help people discover what the Bible says about the topic and how the lesson's point applies to their lives. In these varied activities, class members find answers to the "So what?" question. Through active and interactive learning methods, people will discover the relevance of the Scriptures and commit to growing closer to God.

You may use either one or both of the options in this section. They are designed to stand alone or to work together. Both present the same point in different ways. "For Even Deeper Discussion" questions appear at the end of each activity in this section. Use these questions whenever you feel they might be particularly helpful for your class.

● The **Closing** pulls everything in the lesson together and often funnels the lesson's message into a time of reflection and prayer.

● The **For Extra Time** section is just that. Use it when you've completed the lesson and still have time left or when you've used one Bible Exploration and Application option and don't have time to do the other. Or you might plan to use it instead of another option.

When you put all the sections together, you get a lesson that's fun and easy to teach. Plus, participants will learn truths they'll remember and apply to their daily lives.

About the Questions and Answers . . .

The answers given after discussion questions are responses participants *might* give. They aren't the only answers or the "right" answers. However, you can use them to spark discussion.

Real life doesn't always allow us to give the "right" answers. That's why some of the responses given are negative or controversial. If someone responds negatively, don't be shocked. Accept the person and use the opportunity to explore other perspectives on the issue.

To get more out of your discussions, use follow-up inquiries such as

- Tell me more.
- What do you mean by that?
- What makes you feel that way?

Guidelines for a Successful Adult Class

- **Be a facilitator, not a lecturer.** Apply-It-To-Life Adult Bible Curriculum is student-based rather than teacher-based. Your job is to direct the activities and facilitate the discussions. You become a choreographer of sorts: someone who gets everyone else involved in the discussion and keeps the discussion on track.
- **Teach adults how to form small groups.** Help adults discover the benefits of small-group discussions by assisting them in forming groups of four, three, or two—whatever the activity calls for. Small-group sharing allows for more discussion and involvement by all participants. It's not as threatening or scary to open up to two people as it would be to 20 or 200!

Some leaders decide not to form small groups because they want to hear everybody's ideas. The intention is good, but some people just won't talk in a large group. Use a "report back" time after small-group discussions to gather the best responses from all groups.

When you form small groups, don't always let people choose those right around them. Try creative group-forming methods to help everyone in the class get to know one another. For example, tell class members: find three other people wearing the same color you are; join two other people who like the same music you do; locate three others who shop at the same grocery store you do; find one who was born the same month as you; choose three who like the same season as you, and so on. If you have fun with it, your class will, too!

● **Encourage relationship building.** George Barna, in his insightful book about the church, *The Frog in the Kettle,* explains that adults today have a strong need to develop friendships. In a society of high-tech toys, "personal" computers, and lonely commutes, people long for positive human contact. That's where our church classes and groups can jump in. Help adults form friendships through your class. What's discovered in a classroom setting will be better applied when friends support each other outside the classroom. In fact, the relationships begun in your class may be as important as the truths you help your adults learn.

● **Be flexible.** Sometimes your class will complete every activity in the lesson with great success and wonderful learning. But what should you do if people go off on a tangent? or they get stuck in one of the activities? What if you don't have time to finish the lesson?

Don't panic. People learn best when they are interested and engaged in meaningful discussion, when they move at their own pace. And if you get through even one activity, your class will discover the point for the whole lesson. So relax. It's OK if you don't get everything done. Try to get to the Closing in every lesson, since its purpose is to bring closure to the topic for the week. But if you don't, don't sweat it!

● **Expect the unexpected.** Active learning is an adventure that doesn't always take you where you think you're going. Don't be surprised if things don't go exactly the way you'd planned. Be open to the different directions the Holy Spirit may lead your class. When something goes wrong or an unexpected emotion is aroused, take advantage of this teachable moment. Ask probing questions; follow up on someone's deep need or concern. Those moments are often the best opportunities for learning that come our way.

● **Participate—and encourage participation.** Apply-It-To-Life Adult Bible Curriculum is only as interactive as you and your class make it. Learning arises out of dialogue. People need to grapple with and verbalize their questions and discoveries. Jump into discussions yourself, but don't "take over." Encourage everyone to participate. You can facilitate smooth discussions by using "active listening" responses such as rephrasing and summing up what's been said. If people seem stumped, use the possible responses after each question to spark further discussion. You may feel like a cheerleader at times, but your efforts will be worth it. The more people participate, the more they'll discover God's truths for themselves.

● **Trust the Holy Spirit.** All the previous six guidelines and the instructions in the lessons will be irrelevant if you ignore the presence of God in your classroom. God sent the Holy Spirit as our helper. As you use this curriculum, ask the Holy Spirit to help you facilitate the lessons. And ask the Holy Spirit to direct your class toward God's truth. Trust that God's Spirit can work through each person's discoveries, not just the teacher's.

How to Use This Course

Before the Four-Week Session

- Read the Course Introduction and This Course at a Glance (pp. 13-14).
- Decide how you'll use the art on the Publicity Page (p. 15) to publicize the course. Prepare fliers, newsletter articles, and posters as needed.
- Look at the Fellowship and Outreach Specials (pp. 67-68) and decide which ones you'll use.

Before Each Lesson

- Read the one-sentence Point, the Objectives, and the Bible Basis for the lesson. The Bible Basis provides background information on the lesson's passages and shows how those passages relate to people today.
- Choose which activities you'll use from the lesson. Remember, it's not important to do every activity. Pick the ones that best fit your group and time allotment.
- Gather necessary supplies. They're listed in This Lesson at a Glance.
- Read each section of the lesson. Adjust activities as necessary to fit your class size and meeting room, but be careful not to delete all the activity. People learn best when they're actively involved in the learning process.

Course Introduction: Communication: Enhancing Your Relationships

What's the big deal about communicating clearly? Ask the person who's missed an important meeting because the time was misprinted in a memo. Ask the first-century Roman who thought Christians were cannibals because they spoke of eating Christ's body and drinking his blood. Ask any parent.

We've all enjoyed the benefits of clear communication and suffered the consequences of broken or missed communication. We all know that miscommunication can result in anything from hurt feelings to an international crisis. But when it comes to telling others about the Christian faith, the stakes are eternal.

Effective communication is especially crucial for us as Christians. At the most basic level, we must be able to interact with each other honestly and openly. It's only as we speak clearly and listen carefully that we learn to respect and appreciate one another.

However, we also need to understand our faith and be able to communicate it effectively to others. Although it's unlikely that anyone would accuse today's Christians of cannibalism, clear communication is just as critical now as it was in the early days of the church. When we carelessly toss around "church" terms such as "redemption," "grace," and "born again" (add a hundred more from your denominational glossary), we often confuse and alienate non-Christians. But with careful and clear communication, our message will come through and relationships will be strengthened rather than soured.

This Course at a Glance

Before you dive into the lessons, familiarize yourself with each lesson's point. Then read the Scripture passages.

- Study them as a background to the lessons.
- Use them as a basis for your personal devotions.
- Think about how they relate to people's situations today.

Lesson 1: What Does It Take?

The Point: Authentic communication demands honesty and courage.

Bible Basis: Luke 9:43b-45 and Matthew 15:21-28

Lesson 2: The Lost Art of Listening

The Point: Active listening is essential to clear communication.

Bible Basis: John 18:33-38 and Mark 4:10-12, 21-25

Lesson 3: When Communication Breaks Down

The Point: With God's help, we can heal relationships that have been hurt by misunderstanding and miscommunication.

Bible Basis: Matthew 16:5-12 and John 3:1-13

Lesson 4: Handling Conflict

The Point: Skillful communicators can turn unproductive conflict into positive communication.

Bible Basis: Acts 26:24-32

PUBLICITY PAGE

Grab your congregation's attention! Add the vital details to the ready-made flier below, photocopy it, and use it to advertise this course on improving communication. Insert the flier in your bulletins. Enlarge it to make posters. Splash the art or anything else from this page in newsletters, bulletins, or even on postcards! It's that simple.

*The art from this page is also available on Group's MinistryNet™ computer on-line resource for you to manipulate on your computer. Call **800-447-1070** for information.*

Communication: Enhancing Your Relationships

A four-week adult course on strengthening relationships through clear communication.

COME TO

ON

AT

COME LEARN HOW TO IMPROVE YOUR RELATIONSHIPS BY BECOMING A BETTER COMMUNICATOR!

Communication: Enhancing Your Relationships

Communication: Enhancing Your Relationships

Lesson 1

What Does It Take?

Authentic communication demands honesty and courage.

THE POINT

OBJECTIVES

Participants will

- experience and identify obstacles to genuine communication,
- explore ways to overcome obstacles to communication, and
- practice honest and courageous communication with a partner.

BIBLE BASIS

Look up the Scriptures. Then read the following background sections to see how the passages relate to people today.

LUKE 9:43b-45

In **Luke 9:43b-45,** Jesus tells his disciples that he will be betrayed.

Having just witnessed an impressive display of Jesus' power (driving a demon out of a small boy, Luke 9:37-43a), the disciples are dumbfounded to hear Jesus predict his betrayal into human hands. This is not the first time Jesus has spoken plainly about his approaching rejection and death (see Luke 9:21-22), but still the disciples do not understand.

Luke does not explain why the disciples were unable to grasp the meaning of Jesus' simple declaration, but the context offers several possibilities. On the one hand, God may have concealed the meaning of the saying until the disciples were better able to accept it; Jesus' death, burial, and resurrection may have helped them understand that glory comes *through* suffering (see Luke 9:45). Still, this does not explain the disciples' fear of asking Jesus for a clarification. It seems as though the disciples preferred ignorance to understanding. But why?

In the first place, they, like many other Jews of that time, hoped that God's Anointed One—the Messiah—would defeat the oppressive Romans and re-establish David's kingdom. If Jesus was the Messiah—and they had just confessed that he was (Luke 9:20)—how could he suffer, be rejected, and die? Their assumptions simply did not permit what he appeared to be saying. If Jesus was right, either their identification of him as the Messiah or their expectations of him as Messiah were wrong.

In addition, immediately after Jesus had first spoken about his impending death, he had announced that anyone who wanted to follow him must follow him to the cross (Luke 9:22-24). It seems reasonable to think, then, that the disciples chose not to accept Jesus' words because they feared the implications that they held for them. Whatever the reason, the disciples lacked the courage to overcome the obstacles to authentic communication with Jesus. As a result, their relationships with him failed to reach the depth they could have reached.

MATTHEW 15:21-28

In **Matthew 15:21-28,** a Canaanite woman asks Jesus to heal her daughter.

It is striking and often troubling to modern readers that Jesus appears to be so rude to the Canaanite woman. Yet it was more surprising to those watching the encounter that Jesus would speak to a woman at all, much less a Canaanite woman. Women in first-century Palestine were rarely treated as men's equals, and the Canaanites and the Jews had been religious and political enemies for centuries.

These weren't the only obstacles that threatened to keep this woman from communicating with Jesus: He initially ignored her (Matthew 15:23a); the disciples asked that she be sent away (Matthew 15:23b); then Jesus denied her request (Matthew 15:24) and referred to her as one of "the dogs" (Matthew 15:26). In spite of all this, the Canaanite woman courageously overcame every obstacle, even extending Jesus' possibly insulting metaphor in order to win the help that she sought.

Jesus gave the Canaanite woman a chance to show others how the ears of true faith hear the words of our Lord, even when those words are difficult to hear. Jesus then demonstrated how God blesses people of true courage and faith. Though it's a difficult task, speaking courageously is often rewarded with a positive result. In this case, the Canaanite woman's courageous communication resulted in Jesus' healing of her daughter.

The stakes are high when we communicate with one another. If we follow the Canaanite woman's example, we'll reap the benefits of healthy communication—healthy relationships. If we act like the disciples, we run the risk of living dark, isolated lives, never knowing what others are thinking and feeling, never feeling that others understand us. Instead of tightening family bonds, we may stretch them to the snapping point. Instead of communicating important messages, we may end up alienating co-workers. Instead of building community, we may split churches. Use this lesson to help your class identify common communication barriers and the foundational commitments of successful communication.

This Lesson at a Glance

Section	*Minutes*	*What Participants Will Do*	*Supplies*
Opening	*1 to 3*	**Introduction to the Course**—Learn what today's lesson is about.	
Bible Exploration and Application	*15 to 20*	☐ *Option 1:* **Patterns**—Try to copy a pattern from verbal instructions and read Luke 9:43b-45 and Matthew 15:21-28 in order to identify obstacles to communication.	Bibles, scissors, paper, pencils, "Patterns" handouts (p. 26)
	20 to 30	☐ *Option 2:* **Communication Stories**—Study communication between Jesus and the disciples in Luke 9:43b-45, and Jesus and a Canaanite woman in Matthew 15:21-28.	Bibles, "Communication Stories" handouts (p. 27), scissors
Closing	*up to 10*	**Listening to Concerns**—Share about relationships in which communication is difficult, then pray for each other.	
For Extra Time	*up to 5*	**Say It With Meaning**—Identify unclear language in hymns and discuss obstacles to clearly communicating their faith.	An old hymnal
	up to 5	**According to Mark**—Compare Matthew 15:21-28 and Mark 7:24-30, then talk about how to communicate differently to different audiences.	Bibles

OPENING

Introduction to the Course

(1 to 3 minutes)

As you begin the class, describe what you'll be learning and doing in today's lesson. Use the following statement or your own summary of the main point: **Welcome to the first week of our four-week series on communication. In this series, we're going to focus on improving our communication skills as a means of deepening our relationships with others. We'll do this in a variety of ways. We're going to experience different kinds of communication, talk about our own relationships, study the Bible together, and communicate with and learn from one another.**

We'll start today by discovering together that ▶ we can overcome the obstacles to authentic communication through honesty and courage.

Encourage class members to get involved in the discussions and activities during the study.

BIBLE EXPLORATION AND APPLICATION

☐ OPTION 1: Patterns

(15 to 20 minutes)

Before class, photocopy and cut apart the "Patterns" handout (p. 26). You will need one-half of the handout for every two adults.

If you have more than 10 describers, arrange them into five groups of fairly equal size and assign each group of describers one of the guidelines.

Form pairs and have each pair decide which partner will be a describer and which an artist. While the artists hand out pencils and blank sheets of paper, gather the describers and give half of them the first pattern from the "Patterns" handout and the other half the second pattern. Then assign each describer one of the following guidelines:

- **You may describe the pattern accurately only half of the time.**
- **You must vacillate and give contradictory information.**
- **You may not respond to your partner's questions.**
- **You may do whatever is necessary to describe the pattern.**
- **You may do anything except show your partner the pattern.**

Send describers back to their artists and have pairs sit back-to-back or facing opposite directions.

Say: **Describers, you have two minutes to verbally direct your partners to reproduce the assigned pattern. Artists, listen carefully and ask questions, but recognize that the describers have different patterns to describe and specific guidelines they must follow.**

Have pairs begin the activity. After two minutes, call time and have artists and describers compare their illustrations. Ask:

- **Artists, are you pleased with your partner's description of the pattern? Why or why not?** (Yes, she spoke clearly and responded to my questions; no, sometimes he gave inaccurate information; no, she ignored my questions.)
- **Describers, why didn't you describe your pattern as well as your partner would have liked?** (I tried, but there was too much noise around us; I kept contradicting myself; I was told to be inaccurate.)
- **How are the limitations in this activity like the obstacles to genuine communication we face every day?** (Sometimes people aren't entirely honest; sometimes people send contradictory messages; sometimes we're unable to clarify confusing messages.)

Have each pair join another pair to form a group of four. Have groups read **Luke 9:43b-45** and **Matthew 15:21-28** and discuss the following questions. Ask the questions one at a time, allowing two to three minutes for each discussion.

- **What obstacles to communication were the disciples unable to overcome?** (They didn't understand Jesus but were afraid to ask for clarification; Jesus said something that contradicted what they thought he should say.)
- **What obstacles to communication was the Canaanite woman able to overcome?** (Jesus seemed to insult her, referring to her as a dog; women in that society were not encouraged to speak up.)
- **Why were the disciples unable to overcome the obstacles? Why could the Canaanite woman overcome them?** (They didn't want to hear what Jesus was saying, but she was willing to listen; they were afraid to hear the truth, but she had the courage to do so.)
- **Think about a relationship you have in which genuine communication is often difficult. What obstacles make it tough?** (Sometimes my friend lies; I'm afraid to know the truth about my marriage; I don't always tell my boss what I really think.)
- **What could you do, either as speaker or listener, to overcome these obstacles?** (Listen carefully to my friend and ask clarifying questions when I suspect a

The Greek word for "dogs" in Matthew 15:26-27 is *kunarion.* It is an endearing form of *kuōn,* the regular word for "dog," in the same way that "doggie" is an endearing form of "dog" in English. *Kunarion* probably refers to household pets as opposed to the scavenger dogs that roamed the streets of most ancient cities and villages. In context, it seems that Jesus is likening the woman's people to puppies begging under the table of God's children, Israel.

lie; tell my husband about my fears, then ask him to help me work through them; speak the truth in love to my boss.)

● **What might be some specific benefits of overcoming these obstacles?** (My friend would learn to speak the truth; my husband and I could face our problems openly and together; my boss would trust me more.)

Call groups together and have volunteers share questions or insights with the entire class. Then say: **Improved communication can only mean improved relationships. One of the first steps to improving communication is recognizing obstacles to clear communication. Sometimes we're not honest with ourselves, sometimes we're not totally honest with others, and sometimes we're afraid to engage in genuine dialogue. Whenever we face these obstacles, we need to remind ourselves that authentic communication demands honesty and courage.**

THE POINT

FOR *Even Deeper* DISCUSSION

● Read Luke 9:46-50. How does the disciples' behavior in these verses help explain their failure to understand Jesus' words?

● What did the disciples value more than honest communication with Jesus?

● Why did Jesus place obstacles in the way of the Canaanite woman? To what extent should we follow Jesus' example when we communicate with others?

□ OPTION 2: *Communication Stories*

(20 to 30 minutes)

Before class, photocopy and cut apart the "Communication Stories" handout (p. 27).

Have adults form groups of four. Say: **Let's take a few minutes to learn a little more about each other. Each of you has 30 seconds to tell about your most amusing or most embarrassing experience of miscommunication. It might be something that happened with your kids, your parents, your spouse, a friend, or a co-worker. If possible, identify the cause of the miscommunication. Go.**

After everyone has had a chance to share, have group members number off from one to four. Send the ones to

TEACHER TIP

If your class size is larger than 24 people, further divide each numbered group into two or more smaller groups for this activity.

one corner of the room, the twos to another, and so on. Each group will take a close look at one of this lesson's biblical texts. Give a copy of the **Luke 9:43b-45** section of the "Communication Stories" handout to each person in the ones and twos and a copy of the **Matthew 15:21-28** section to each person in the threes and fours.

Instruct groups to read and follow the handout instructions. After about 10 minutes, have adults return to their original foursomes. Have each class member present two important truths or applications from his or her passage to the members of the foursome. After about five minutes, direct groups to briefly discuss the following questions, reporting back to the whole class what they discussed after each question. (If the class completed the "Patterns" activity, omit the first question). Ask:

- **What were the primary obstacles to communication in the biblical passages you studied?** (The disciples didn't want to hear what Jesus had to say; the Canaanite woman had to defy ethnic division, social expectations, and hostility.)
- **What made the Canaanite woman a better communicator than the disciples?** (The woman courageously overcame the obstacles that she faced; the disciples valued their own comfort over honest communication.)
- **What are the differences between the communication skills of the Canaanite woman and those of the disciples?** (The Canaanite woman spoke her mind; the disciples were too afraid of being wrong.)
- **What can we learn from these passages about the demands of genuine communication?** (It's important to speak courageously; we need to be willing to hear what the other is saying.)
- **How can we be more honest and courageous at home? at work? with our friends?** (I can tell my husband when he hurts my feelings; I can explain to my wife why I'm unhappy; I can admit to my supervisor that I don't understand; I can confront my friend's hypocrisy.)

Say: **When the Canaanite woman spoke honestly and courageously, Jesus understood and met her needs. When the disciples neglected to voice their questions about Jesus' troubling message, they went away confused and possibly frustrated with Jesus and themselves. While the Canaanite woman's relationship with Jesus was deepened, the disciples' relationship with him was damaged by their lack of honesty and courage, which are vital to authentic communication.**

The English word "Christ" comes from the Greek word *Christos,* which means "anointed one," while the English word "Messiah" stems from the Hebrew word for "anointed one," *meshiach.* In ancient Israel, *meshiach* generally refers to the king, who was anointed with oil as a sign of divine selection (1 Samuel 10:1; 16:13; 1 Kings 1:39). Even after the fall of the Davidic kingdom in 587 B.C., Jews trusted God to establish David's kingdom forever (2 Samuel 7:11b-16) and thus eagerly awaited the coming of the Anointed One. They expected the Messiah to set up an earthly kingdom and free them from foreign (Roman) domination.

THE POINT

FOR *Even Deeper* DISCUSSION

● Who concealed Jesus' words from the disciples (Luke 9:45)? Why might they have been concealed?

● To what extent are the disciples responsible for failing to understand Jesus? To what extent might God be responsible?

● What does the story about the Canaanite woman teach about church fellowship? How might we apply this to our church?

The "Apply-It-To-Life This Week" handout (p. 28) helps people further explore the issues uncovered in today's class. Give everyone a photocopy of the handout. Encourage class members to take time during the coming week to explore the questions and activities listed on the handout.

CLOSING

Listening to Concerns

(up to 10 minutes)

Have each person turn to a nearby partner and have partners take turns talking about a relationship in which communication is often difficult. Encourage adults to practice honesty and courage as they identify the primary obstacles to authentic communication in their relationships and what they can do to overcome those obstacles.

Then have partners pray for each other, specifically naming the relationships and asking God to help break down the obstacles. Close the prayer time with a prayer similar to this one: **Dear God, we thank you for the many ways you communicate with us. Help us to see you working in our lives and answering our prayers. ▶ And empower us to be honest and courageous communicators so we can build healthy relationships in which authentic communication takes place. In Jesus' name, amen.**

THE POINT ▶

For Extra Time

SAY IT WITH MEANING
(up to 5 minutes)

Get a copy of an old church hymnal and read some of the more difficult or archaic phrases to the class. Ask class members how well these hymns communicate their feelings about their faith. Then have class members list words and attitudes that often become obstacles when they try to communicate their faith to others. Close by having people explain how they can overcome these obstacles to authentic communication.

ACCORDING TO MARK
(up to 5 minutes)

Form groups of four to look up and read Mark 7:24-30, which is a parallel to Matthew's story about the Canaanite woman. Have groups compare the two versions of the story and try to explain the differences between them. Discuss how people's audiences and purposes should influence the way they communicate.

Patterns

PATTERN #1:

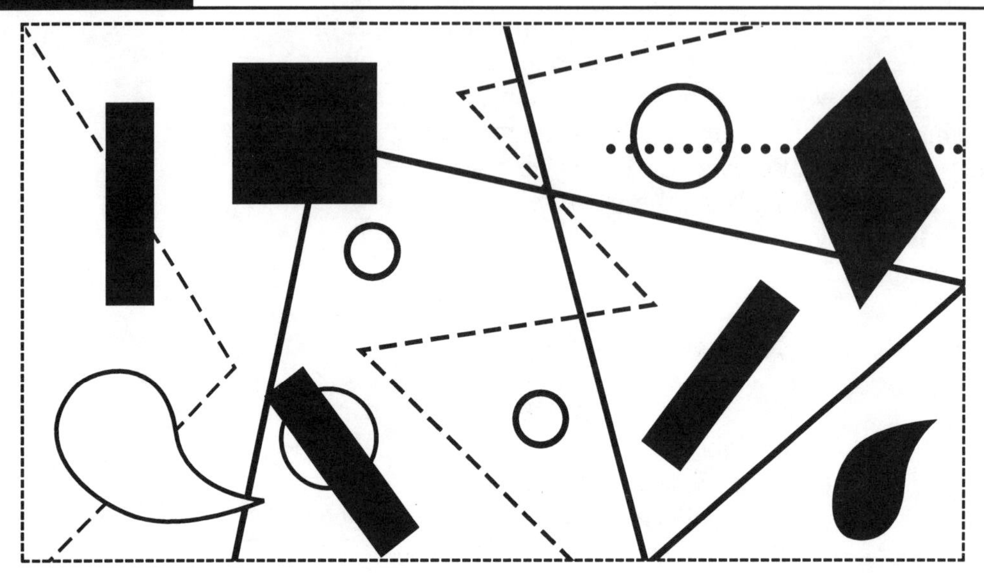

PATTERN #2:

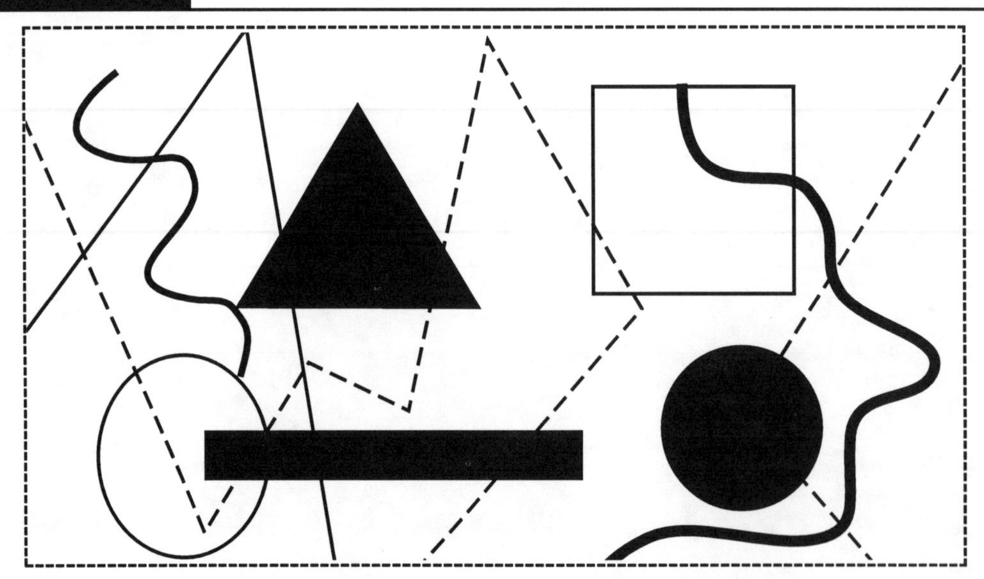

Communication Stories

LUKE 9:43b-45

Read Luke 9:43b-45 and this background information. Then answer the questions below.

After Peter confesses that Jesus is the Messiah (Luke 9:18-20), he and some of the other disciples witness two extraordinary displays of power that seem to confirm their faith confession: Jesus' transfiguration (Luke 9:28-36) and the casting out of a demon (Luke 9:37-43a). Then Jesus reminds them (Luke 9:21-22) that he will be delivered into the hands of mere mortals. The disciples do not understand Jesus' saying and are afraid to ask him to clarify it.

- Why are the disciples afraid to ask for clarification: Are they afraid of appearing ignorant? Do they prefer not to understand? Is there some other explanation?
- Read the FYI section below. Why might the disciples prefer not to understand Jesus?
- Read Luke 9:23-24 and answer the previous question again.
- How do we sometimes act like the disciples and avoid honest communication with others?
- How can we improve communication when people don't want to understand us? when we are afraid to understand?

FYI The English word "Christ" derives from the Greek word *Christos,* which means "anointed one." The English word "Messiah" derives from the Hebrew word for "anointed one," *meshiach.* In ancient Israel, the king was anointed with oil as a sign of God's selection. During New Testament times, many Jews expected an "anointed one" to defeat the Romans and re-establish David's kingdom.

MATTHEW 15:21-28

Read Matthew 15:21-28 and this background information. Then answer the questions below.

As a member of an ethnic group despised by most Jews, the Canaanite woman had little reason to expect a Jew like Jesus to speak with her. In addition, her culture discouraged women from standing up and making themselves heard. To make matters worse, the disciples wanted her sent away and Jesus himself ignored and apparently insulted her. Still, the woman persisted and eventually won Jesus' approval and assistance.

- What motivated the Canaanite woman to persevere? What personal characteristics enabled her to overcome the obstacles to communication?
- Read the FYI section at the end of the handout. Why do you think Jesus implied that the woman was one of the dogs?
- The Canaanite woman accepted and even used Jesus' metaphor about tossing the children's bread to the dogs. What can we learn from her example?
- What obstacles to genuine communication did you face this past week? How did you or could you have overcome them?

FYI The Greek word "dogs" in Matthew 15:26-27 is *kunarion.* It is an endearing form of *kuōn,* the regular word for "dog," in the same way that "doggie" is an endearing form of "dog" in English. *Kunarion* probably refers to household pets as opposed to the scavengers that roamed the streets of most ancient cities and villages. So, although Jesus' reference to the woman as one of the "dogs" is far from flattering, it is not as insulting as it might first appear.

LESSON 1

What Does It Take?

The Point: ▶ Authentic communication demands honesty and courage.
Scripture Focus: Luke 9:43b-45 and Matthew 15:21-28

Reflecting on God's Word

Each day this week, read one of the following Scripture passages and examine what it says about honest and courageous communication. Then examine how well you are applying the message of the passage in your life. You may want to list your discoveries in the space under each passage.

Day 1: James 3:1-12. Our words can do great harm or great good.

Day 2: Proverbs 12:22; 19:22. An honest person is valued by God and by others.

Day 3: Matthew 15:10-20. Our conversations reveal our inner selves.

Day 4: Colossians 4:2-6. We should speak boldly and wisely.

Day 5: Colossians 3:15-17. Our speech should build others up.

Day 6: Matthew 5:33-37. We should never break a promise.

Beyond Reflection

1. Read the book of Jonah (it's just four chapters long!) and think about the following questions:

- What was at stake for the people of Nineveh? for God?
- What obstacles stood in the way of genuine communication between Jonah and the people of Nineveh?
- How effective was Jonah as a communicator of God's message?
- How are we often like Jonah in our relationships with others?

2. Interview at least three people in various life stages about the role communication has played in their relationships. Ask questions such as

- What is the most difficult aspect of communicating with others?
- How has the nature of your communication with friends changed over the years you've known them?
- What's an important communication tip you wish everyone knew?

Next Week's Bible Passages: John 18:33-38 and Mark 4:10-12, 21-25

Lesson 2

The Lost Art of Listening

Active listening is essential to clear communication.

THE POINT

Objectives

Participants will

- describe active listening in terms of attitude and skills,
- evaluate the interaction between Jesus and Pilate,
- discover what Jesus says about the demands of active listening, and
- practice active listening in communication.

Bible Basis

Look up the Scriptures. Then read the following background sections to see how the passages relate to people today.

JOHN 18:33-38

John 18:33-38 records a part of Jesus' trial: his initial hearing before Pilate.

A great deal happened within a few hours of Judas' betrayal (John 18:1-11). First Jesus was questioned by Annas, the former high priest (John 18:12-13, 19-24). Then he was sentenced to death by Caiaphas, the current high priest, and the Jewish council of elders (Mark 14:53-65). Eventually he appeared before Pilate, the Roman governor of the province of Judea. Of course, the hearing before Pilate would alter nothing. Jesus' fate was certain regardless of what Pilate thought or did (John 18:38b-40; 19:4, 6, 12).

So why did John take the time to narrate the hearing? What should we learn from his telling? In the first place, John emphasizes Jesus' innocence. Pilate was an unbiased third party who weighed the religious leaders' accusations against Jesus' testimony (John 18:29-30, 35-38) and concluded that Jesus was not guilty of any crime (John 18:38b). However, this doesn't mean that Pilate understood Jesus. In fact, John implies that Jesus' talk of a kingdom "not of this world" and of being "on the side of truth" left Pilate uncertain and confused. Apparently John wants the reader to learn from Pilate's example that one must go beyond the facts about Jesus and understand the man himself.

Many of the barriers that kept Pilate from comprehending what Jesus was saying also make it difficult for us to communicate with one another. Pilate interpreted "kingdom" and "truth" from his own context and perspective when he should have tried to discern what Jesus meant by these terms. In addition, some of Pilate's questions advanced clearer communication, but others intentionally subverted it. Finally, it seems that Pilate decided that talking with Jesus was simply too much work, so he ended the conversation with a dead-end question: "What is truth?"

MARK 4:10-12, 21-25

In **Mark 4:10-12, 21-25,** Jesus teaches that listening is important.

It's commonly assumed that Jesus taught in parables because they provided the most effective means of communicating his ideas. However, that assumption runs counter to Jesus' declaration that he told parables to conceal his message (Mark 4:10-12).

Although Jesus' statement sounds strange at first, it makes sense in the immediate context. After Jesus told the parable of the sower (Mark 4:3-8), he challenged his audience to pay attention to what he was saying. But no one seemed to get it. Even his disciples wondered about his parables. In response, Jesus explained that he told parables so that "those on the outside" might see without perceiving and hear without understanding (Mark 4:12, quoting Isaiah 6:9-10). In short, Jesus didn't want certain people to understand what he was saying.

Of course this would seem to make Jesus responsible for the failed communication, but Jesus argues otherwise. In the first place, just as no one would light a lamp and keep it covered up, Jesus did not use parables in order to *keep* his message hidden (Mark 4:21). Rather, he *temporarily* veiled his message so that only those who had "ears to hear" would hear it (Mark 4:22-23). Jesus used parables to ensure that only those eager to hear him would be able to understand him fully. Jesus wanted to be heard, but only by those serious about carrying on a real, life-changing conversation (Mark 4:24-25).

We can learn a great deal about listening from this text.

First, the listener is just as responsible for clear communication as the speaker is. We must be open to hear what the speaker has to say. In addition, listening takes effort. We must not expect conversation to be easy. Sometimes we need to endure just to earn the right to be heard. Finally, insincere or half-hearted listening can cost us dearly both in our relationships with others and in our relationship with God.

Our ability to listen affects every aspect of our lives, but few of us do it as well as we could. In fact, we're better at *pretending* to pay attention to our children, spouses, friends, and co-workers than we are at actually *listening* to them. Unfortunately, we don't hear God very well either. God speaks to us in various ways—through other people, through events in our lives, through the Bible, and during our times of prayer and meditation on his Word—but all too often we fail to hear his voice. This lesson will help adults learn how to listen actively so they can become more effective communicators.

This Lesson at a Glance

Section	*Minutes*	*What Participants Will Do*	*Supplies*
Opening	*up to 10*	**Listening to One Another**—Learn what today's lesson is about and experience what it's like not to be listened to.	
Bible Exploration and Application	*15 to 20*	☐ *Option 1:* **I Heard What You Said**—Summarize what another group member says, then discuss active listening and John 18:33-38.	Bibles
	25 to 30	☐ *Option 2:* **Perspectives**—Share pleasant memories; practice actively listening to John 18:33-38 and Mark 4:10-12, 21-25; and discuss how they can listen more actively.	Bibles, pencils, "What I Hear You Saying Is . . ." handouts (p. 40)
Closing	*up to 10*	**If They Would Listen**—Tell what they would say to someone if they knew he or she would truly listen.	
For Extra Time	*up to 5*	**Red Flags**—Discuss how people inside and outside of the church misunderstand each other.	
	up to 5	**Story Time**—Listen actively to a story shared by a class member.	

OPENING

Listening to One Another

(up to 10 minutes)

As you begin the class, describe what you'll be learning and doing in today's lesson. Use the following statement or your own summary of the main point: **Welcome to the second week in our series on communication. Last week we learned that authentic communication demands honesty and courage on the part of the speaker. Today we're going to explore what communication requires of listeners. Perhaps the easiest way to get started is to listen to one another.**

Form pairs. Say: **Have the partner who's had the most unusual trip take two minutes to tell his or her partner about that trip. Listening partners, however, must avoid eye contact, face another direction, and show no indication of actually listening to the story.**

After two minutes, call time and have partners switch roles for two more minutes.

Then have each pair join another pair to form a foursome. Have group members take turns answering the following questions. Ask volunteers to share their groups' insights with the whole class after each question. Ask:

- **How did this activity make you feel? Explain.** (Uncomfortable, I really wanted to make eye contact; awkward, it didn't seem polite to look away; strange, I felt like I was talking to myself.)
- **How well did you hear your partner?** (I listened carefully at the beginning, but my mind wandered the last minute; I had a hard time focusing on my partner; I understood the words, but I wondered what my partner's facial expressions were.)
- **In everyday life, how have you played the two roles you just experienced in this activity?** Answers will vary.
- **Based on what we've learned in this activity, how can we actively listen to others?** (We can make eye contact; we can nod in agreement when we understand, we can face and observe the person.)

Say: **Listening is more than having our ears open to the sounds and words that float our way. As we'll discover today, the active listening that is essential to clear communication demands the engagement of our whole selves.**

THE POINT

Bible Exploration and Application

☐ **Option 1:**

I Heard What You Said

(15 to 20 minutes)

Form groups of four. Have group members choose a topic that interests them, such as politics, music, sports, or relationships. Encourage people to choose a topic of some interest to *all* group members.

Say: **You're going to have five minutes to talk about the subject your group has chosen. But there is one rule everyone must follow: Before each of you speaks, you must summarize the statement of the person who spoke immediately before you. This must be done to the satisfaction of that person. When you're ready, you may begin. The first person to talk about the subject must first recap the rules I've just stated. Go.**

After five minutes, call time. Ask:

- **What was it like to listen to others carefully? to be listened to carefully?** (It took effort, but it was worth it; I discovered that I don't listen that well; since people were really listening, I chose my words carefully; I felt that my opinions were important.)

Say: **Summarizing or restating what someone says to you is one way to listen actively, but there are many others.**

Instruct groups to discuss the following questions one at a time. Allow interaction time, then have groups share their answers with the whole class. Ask:

- **What did your group members do that showed you they were listening?** (They asked questions to clarify things they didn't fully understand; they nodded when they agreed with me; they looked me in the eyes.)
- **What other active listening skills can help us hear others more accurately?** (We can observe the other person's body language; we can tune out distractions; we can focus our attention on what the person is saying and not on what we want to say.)
- **Why do we sometimes fail to listen actively?** (We're too busy trying to state our own opinions; we're distracted by someone or something else; we don't think that the speaker is saying anything important.)
- **What are some results of not listening actively?** (We make our conversation partners feel unimportant; we misunderstand what's being said; we miss important information.)
- **What are the benefits of practicing active learning?** (We learn more about others; we clarify things that

To help class members discover the variety of ways they can practice active listening, list their answers on a piece of newsprint titled "Active Listening Skills."

may be unclear; we communicate respect and concern; we improve our relationships with others.)

Instruct groups to read **John 18:33-38** then to discuss the following questions. Give groups time to read the passage, then ask:

- **What active listening techniques did Pilate use?** (He asked Jesus questions; he met with Jesus face to face; he asked Jesus to clarify what he meant.)
- **How well did Pilate understand Jesus?** (Pilate didn't know what kind of kingdom Jesus was talking about; Pilate realized that Jesus was innocent of treason; Pilate didn't understand who Jesus was.)
- **What were the results of Pilate's not understanding Jesus as well as he could have?** (He didn't learn more about Jesus' kingdom; he was unable to explain or defend Jesus' innocence; he missed an opportunity to understand the truth.)
- **What could Pilate have done to understand Jesus better?** (He could have asked Jesus to describe his kingdom further; he could have requested that Jesus clarify what it means to be on the side of truth; he could have continued the conversation until he got to know Jesus better.)
- **How can you become a more active listener at home? on the job?** (I can turn off the television when my kids want to talk; I can look directly at my spouse when we talk; I can ask my supervisor to clarify instructions.)
- **What will be the likely benefits of listening more actively?** (My kids and I will understand one another better; my spouse will feel important and respected; my supervisor will know that I care about doing the job correctly.)

Read **Mark 4:23-24a,** then say: **There's nothing complicated about active listening. It's really nothing more than paying close attention to your conversation partner. We practice active listening by making eye contact, asking questions, observing body language, or even restating what someone says to make sure we heard it correctly. Whatever form it takes, we need to remember that active listening is an essential element of clear and meaningful communication.**

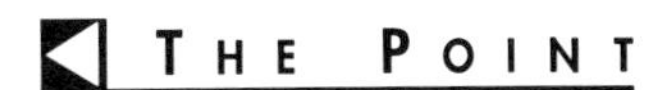

FOR *Even Deeper* DISCUSSION

● What social, religious, economic, and political differences might have made it difficult for Pilate to understand Jesus? How could Pilate have overcome those obstacles?

● How do these kinds of obstacles keep us from understanding others?

● How does God speak to us today? How can we practice active listening in our relationship with God? What keeps us from hearing God as well as we could?

TEACHER TIP

If you used the "I Heard What You Said" activity, you may want to form new foursomes in this activity so adults have a chance to move around and interact with other people.

Encourage class members to practice active listening while others speak. In addition, be sure to model active listening at every opportunity, but especially while the reporters share their groups' insights with the class.

THE POINT ▶

☐ OPTION 2: *Perspectives*

(25 to 30 minutes)

Before class, make one copy of the "What I Hear You Saying Is…" handout (p. 40) for each person.

Form groups of four. Say: **Let's do some active listening. Each group member has two minutes to recount his or her most treasured memory. Listening group members are to practice as many active-listening techniques as possible. For example, they should do things such as focus on the speaker, observe his or her body language, ask clarifying questions, and recap what he or she says. Go.**

After everyone has had a chance to share, ask:

● **How did it feel to know that people were really listening to your best memory?** (It was great because I love talking about my daughter's birth; generally I'm shy, but knowing that everyone was listening helped me open up; it was a little scary, but the listeners made me feel important.)

After groups discuss the question, give each class member a copy of the "What I Hear You Saying Is…" handout and a pencil. Say: ▶ **Active listening is essential to clear communication in our everyday conversations, but it's also helpful in other areas. For example, we read the Bible with greater understanding when we pay close attention to its words, summarize what we think it says, and ask questions about things that are unclear. Let's take some time to practice that with the "What I Hear You Saying Is . . . " handout. Follow the directions on the handout. After about 15 minutes, everyone will get a chance to share insights with the rest of the class.**

After approximately 15 minutes, call time and direct the group reporters to share their groups' findings from each of the three sections on the handout. After every group has reported, have adults discuss the following questions in their groups. Have groups share discoveries or additional questions. Ask:

- **According to Jesus, what attitudes are foundational to active listening?** (We need to value what the speaker is saying; we must be committed to understanding the other person; we must be willing to make the effort to overcome obstacles to communication.)
- **What does Jesus imply is the goal of active listening?** (To comprehend what the speaker means; to understand the speaker's perspective; to "connect" with the other person.)
- **What is one way you can be a more active listener this week at home? at work?** (I can set aside what I'm doing when my spouse starts a conversation; I can ask my kids to clarify what they mean instead of just reacting to what they say; I can try to hear things from my supervisor's perspective.)
- **How does this statement apply to our biblical passages and to our lives: "Seek first to understand, then to be understood"?** (Pilate should have put aside his perspective to understand Jesus better; we must understand the speaker's perspective before we respond with our own; we need to remember that the goal is real communication, not just stating our own opinions.)

Say: **Active listening is both an attitude and a skill. So if we're serious about communicating more effectively with others, we need to commit ourselves to understanding them. Then we need to practice the skills that will enable us to hear them accurately. ▶ Active listening is essential to the kind of communication that will strengthen our relationships, so we must make a constant effort not only to speak honestly and courageously but also to listen actively.**

BIBLE INSIGHT

The wording of Pilate's question in John 18:38 is consistent with the typical Greek definition of truth as a set of facts derived from intellectual effort. According to John, Jesus taught that truth is both factual *and* relational. On the one hand, certain facts are true because they describe the way things really are (John 8:44-46; 16:13; 17:17). However, truth is also an attribute of God. Jesus came from God the Father to reveal God to humans (John 1:17-18). Jesus was "the truth" (John 14:6). Had Pilate recognized this, he might have asked a different question.

◀ THE POINT

FOR *Even Deeper* DISCUSSION

- What was Pilate's goal when he talked to Jesus? What was Jesus' goal?
- How do differing goals make communication difficult? How can we overcome this obstacle to communication?
- According to Mark 4:10-12, 15-21, Jesus made it difficult for some people to understand his message. Is it ever appropriate for us to make it difficult to understand? Explain.

The "Apply-It-To-Life This Week" handout (p. 41) helps people further explore the issues uncovered in today's class. Give everyone a photocopy of the handout. Encourage class members to take time out during the coming week to explore the questions and activities listed on the handout.

CLOSING

If They Would Listen

(up to 5 minutes)

Have adults remain in their groups of four. Ask them to think about what they would say and to whom they would say it, if they were sure that their message would be carefully listened to and understood. Then have people share their messages with their group members.

Be sensitive to those who may feel uncomfortable sharing what they'd like to say. If they don't feel comfortable saying the names of the people they'd like to speak to, that's OK. Encourage adults to speak with honesty and courage and to listen with active, caring support.

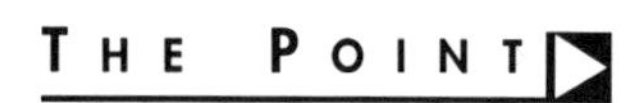

After five minutes, say: **Although we can't guarantee that we will always be understood, we can do a lot to understand others. And our commitment of careful, active listening may motivate others to listen carefully, too. Let's close in silent prayer, first thanking God that ▶ active listening can make us better communicators, then spending a moment listening to what God might say to us today.**

For Extra Time

RED FLAGS

(up to 5 minutes)

Have class members call out religious words or phrases that people outside of the church often misunderstand. Ask adults how they feel when others form negative opinions of them on the basis of these misunderstandings. Then have people give examples of how church people misunderstand words or phrases that people outside of the church use. Ask how this misunderstanding affects their relationships with those people. Close by challenging adults to listen carefully to those who may not hold the same beliefs that they do.

STORY TIME
(up to 5 minutes)

To allow adults an opportunity to practice active listening, have a volunteer share with the class a story about his or her life. At the conclusion of the story, ask class members to recap the main elements of the story. Ask:

- **Where did the story take place?**
- **Who was involved?**
- **What happened?**
- **When did it happen?**
- **How did the story make you feel?**

What I Hear You Saying Is . . .

Learn three keys to active listening. You have five minutes to complete each section. Choose one person to be a reader, a second to be a recorder who will write down the group's conclusions, a third to be a reporter who will share the group's insights with the class, and a fourth to be an encourager who will keep everyone involved and the discussion on track.

1. **Summarize**
   Read John 18:33-38.
   Now summarize the key points of Jesus' responses by answering these questions:
   - What are the characteristics of Jesus' kingdom? How is it different from the one Pilate had in mind?
   - Read the FYI section below. What does Jesus mean when he says, "Everyone on the side of truth listens to me"?
   - What was at the core of the communication problem between Pilate and Jesus?

FYI Pilate seems to think that truth is a set of facts that can be learned (John 18:38). According to John, Jesus taught that truth is both factual *and* relational. On the one hand, certain teachings are true because they describe the way things really are (John 17:17). However, truth is also an attribute of God. Jesus came from the Father as a personal revelation of God. He was "the truth" (John 14:6).

2. **Question**
   People ask questions for a variety of reasons:
   - to discover information,
   - to clarify,
   - to make a point,
   - to redirect the conversation.

   Read John 18:33-38 and state the purpose of each question.
   Now discuss:
   - To what extent did Pilate's questions help him understand Jesus better?
   - What questions could Pilate have asked to understand Jesus better?

3. **Pay Attention**
   Read Mark 4:10-12, 21-25.
   Answer the following questions to discover the nature of true listening.
   - Jesus explains in Mark 4:10-12 that he spoke in parables to conceal his message from some people. How does Mark 4:21-22 clarify what he means?
   - Why were some people able to understand Jesus when others were not?
   - What does Mark 4:24b-25 teach about the listener's responsibility in communication?

LESSON 2

The Lost Art of Listening

The Point: ▶ Active listening is essential to clear communication.
Scripture Focus: John 18:33-38 and Mark 4:10-12, 21-25

Reflecting on God's Word

Each day this week, read one of the following Scripture passages and examine what it teaches about the importance of listening. Then examine how well you're applying the passage in your life. You may want to list your discoveries in the space under each passage.

Day 1: Proverbs 12:15. Listening is a sign of wisdom.

Day 2: Jeremiah 5:21-31. God demands that his people listen to him.

Day 3: James 1:22-25. Listening must be accompanied by acting.

Day 4: Proverbs 18:13. Listening is more important than speaking.

Day 5: John 10:25-30. Those who listen to Jesus gain eternal life.

Day 6: Proverbs 15:31-32. The wise listen when others correct them.

Beyond Reflection

1. Listening is an important biblical concept. Yet it seems that God's people didn't always listen to God's messengers. It's no surprise that God sometimes sent a message in concise commands that no one could misinterpret. Such instances are found in Matthew 17:1-8; Mark 9:2-8; and Luke 9:28-36. Read all three passages and examine the differences in the accounts of the Transfiguration (the transformation of Jesus to show his heavenly glory).

- What remains the same in these three accounts? What is different?
- What did God want the disciples to hear when he commanded them to listen to Jesus?
- What kept the disciples from hearing Jesus' words?

2. Use a concordance to look up Bible passages containing words such as "listen," "voice," and "hear." Explore the various means that God uses to communicate to his people.

Next Week's Bible Passages: Matthew 16:5-12 and John 3:1-13

Lesson 3

When Communication Breaks Down

THE POINT

With God's help, we can heal relationships that have been hurt by misunderstanding and miscommunication.

OBJECTIVES

Participants will

- discover how and why communication breaks down,
- explore misunderstandings recorded in the Bible, and
- identify ways to heal relationships that have been hurt by miscommunication.

BIBLE BASIS

Look up the Scriptures. Then read the following background sections to see how the passages relate to people today.

MATTHEW 16:5-12

Matthew 16:5-12 records Jesus' warning about the influence of the Pharisees and Sadducees.

The 12 disciples often appear comedic in their attempts to understand Jesus. This episode is no exception. Here the disciples focus so much on the circumstances of the moment that they miss the bigger picture.

After Jesus rejected the Pharisees and Sadducees' request for a sign from heaven, he and his disciples started to cross the Sea of Galilee. Unfortunately, the disciples had forgotten to bring bread. So when Jesus warned them to beware of the Jewish religious leaders' yeast, they thought he meant that they were not to take bread from the religious leaders; they were to suffer the consequences of their own forgetfulness and go without.

Of course, Jesus was not worried about bread. He had already provided more than enough bread for thousands (Matthew 14:13-21; 15:29-39). Jesus wanted his disciples to be careful of the teaching of the Pharisees and Sadducees—the demand for a sign from heaven when they were surrounded by signs on earth. Eventually Jesus' disciples understood, but only after Jesus turned their eyes from the literal object to its metaphorical meaning (compare Mark 8:14-21).

Like the disciples, we often make wrong assumptions about what others are saying. It happens in our Bible reading and our day-to-day conversations. All too often, we focus on the literal facts and forget to consider their theological or symbolic significance. This passage reminds us that understanding often requires us to look beyond the words to the ideas they represent.

JOHN 3:1-13

In **John 3:1-13** Jesus tells Nicodemus that he must be born from above.

The encounter between Jesus and Nicodemus communicates an important message to all people: Only those who experience spiritual birth will enter God's kingdom. However, it also reveals how easy it is to focus so much on the physical and the literal that one misses the spiritual significance of what's being said.

Nicodemus and Jesus were both teachers (John 3:2, 10), but this did not guarantee smooth and effortless communication. While Jesus taught about entering God's kingdom through spiritual birth, Nicodemus thought about entering his mother's womb for a second physical birth. When Jesus likened the workings of the Spirit to the wind, Nicodemus became incredulous. Nicodemus didn't recognize that Jesus was using physical phenomena such as entrance, birth, and wind to speak of spiritual realities (John 3:3, 5-8). Nicodemus didn't realize that he needed to look beyond his normal field of vision to comprehend what Jesus was saying.

Unfortunately, sometimes communication breaks down even when people want to understand each other. Sometimes honest and courageous speaking and active listening are simply not enough. The results of miscommunication may range from temporary confusion to hurt feelings to broken relationships. This lesson will help adults explore the causes of miscommunication and discover ways to heal relationships injured by misunderstanding.

This Lesson at a Glance

Section	*Minutes*	*What Participants Will Do*	*Supplies*
Opening	*up to 10*	**Get the Message**—Alter a message as it's passed around and learn what today's lesson is about.	Paper, pencils
Bible Exploration and Application	*20 to 30*	☐ *Option 1:* **Misunderstandings**—Study misunderstandings in Matthew 16:5-12 and John 3:1-13 and discuss times they've been misunderstood.	Bibles, "Misunderstandings" handouts (p. 53)
	15 to 20	☐ *Option 2:* **Healing the Hurts**—Rip up and mend paper "relationships," then explore biblical principles for mending relationships.	Bibles, paper, pencils, transparent tape
Closing	*up to 10*	**Different Worlds**—Discover how different they are from one another.	Paper, pencils
For Extra Time	*up to 5*	**Through Your Eyes**—Discuss how their experiences affect how they communicate.	
	up to 5	**Discovering Prejudices**—Evaluate how prejudices affect the way they hear others.	

OPENING

Get the Message

(up to 10 minutes)

Before class, copy the following message on a sheet of paper: "Sometimes I'm clearer than others."

To begin class, give each person a sheet of paper and a pencil. Then say: **So far in our series on communication, we've learned that genuine communication demands honesty and courage of speakers and the active engagement of listeners. As we put these principles into practice, we will be better communicators. However, we'll never be immune to miscommunication.**

TEACHER **TIP**

If your class is larger than 10, form groups of 10 or fewer for this activity. Have each group complete the activity independently.

Hand the paper with the message on it to someone near you. Then say: **We're going to pass this message around the room. When you get it, read the message, then change just one word and write the new message on your paper. Then pass the new message to someone else. We'll continue until everyone's had a chance to change the message.**

Collect the final version of the sentence and read it aloud. Then read aloud the original sentence. Form groups of five and have them discuss the following questions. Ask volunteers to share their groups' insights with the whole class. Ask:

- **How is the way our sentence changed like the way communication breaks down in everyday life?** (People pass along only part of the story; people paraphrase things, but they may mean something different to someone else.)
- **What are the consequences of misunderstanding and miscommunication?** (People are hurt; things don't get accomplished; relationships are strained.)

THE POINT ▶

Say: **In this activity, we deliberately caused a communication breakdown. But communication often breaks down without our intent. So today we're going to explore how and why communication breaks down and ▶ discover ways to heal relationships hurt by misunderstanding or miscommunication.**

Encourage class members to get involved in the discussions and activities during the study.

BIBLE EXPLORATION AND APPLICATION

☐ **OPTION 1:**

Misunderstandings

(20 to 30 minutes)

Before class, make one copy of the "Misunderstandings" handout (p. 53) for each person.

Form groups of four. Then say: **I'd like each of you to take one minute to tell your group members the most affirming thing anyone has ever said to you.**

After everyone has shared, have adults answer the following questions in their groups. Ask:

- **How did that person's affirmation affect your relationship with him or her?** (Since I felt accepted, I was more willing to accept my friend; it gave me the courage to share some personal feelings; I looked for opportunities to encourage my friend.)
- **Can you describe a time someone tried to say something nice to you and somehow messed up?** Answers will vary.
- **How did that miscommunication affect your relationship with that person?** (We laughed about it and moved on; both my friend and I were embarrassed; I was hurt, but I tried to pretend that I wasn't.)

Say: **It's always nice when someone makes the effort to say something that makes us feel good. Unfortunately, sometimes even the best intentions get mangled in translation. Time and time again miscommunication injures people and damages relationships. Let's examine several biblical accounts to gain some insight into how and why miscommunication takes place.**

Instruct each group to number off from one to four. Send the ones to one area of the room, the twos to another, and so on. Give a copy of the "Misunderstandings" handout to each adult, then assign the ones and twos **Matthew 16:5-12** and the threes and fours **John 3:1-13.** Tell groups to follow the instructions accompanying their assigned passages.

After about 10 minutes, direct adults to rejoin their original groups and explain to one another what their biblical passages teach about the causes of miscommunication. Remind people to practice active listening during this time.

After about five minutes, have class members discuss the following questions in their groups. Ask:

- **What causes misunderstanding?** (People hear what they want to hear; people focus on being understood, not on understanding; people care more about their feelings than about communicating.)
- **How do people normally react when they misunderstand? when they are misunderstood?** (They pretend to understand; they redirect the conversation; they become defensive; they stop trying to communicate.)
- **Think back to your most recent communication breakdown, either when you were misunderstood or when you misunderstood someone else. What caused the misunderstanding?** Answers will vary.

BIBLE INSIGHT

With a little help, anyone can interpret a metaphor such as that found in Matthew 16:6. First, identify what the object (yeast) refers to (teachings). Then explain what the object implies about what it refers to. In this case, Jesus warns the disciples that the teachings of the Pharisees and Sadducees can affect them just as yeast affects dough. Like yeast, the teaching can become a hidden influence that spreads into every area of their lives.

BIBLE INSIGHT

Nicodemus' misunderstanding of Jesus was caused by several things. First, Jesus and Nicodemus used the same words to refer to different realities. Jesus spoke of spiritual birth and entering the kingdom of God; Nicodemus talked of physical birth and entering his mother's womb. In addition, Jesus used some ambiguous words that made (and make!) understanding difficult. The Greek word *anōthen* means both "from above" and "again" (John 3:3, 7, 31). Apparently Jesus intended the former, but Nicodemus heard the latter (3:4). Moreover, *pneuma* can refer either to "wind" or "the Spirit" (3:8). Finally, it is unclear whether "water" in 3:5 refers to baptism, physical birth, or the Holy Spirit (John 1:33; 7:37-39; Ezekiel 36:25-26).

● **How did the miscommunication affect your relationship with that person?** (It created false expectations about our relationship; we became frustrated with each other; I stopped opening up to my friend.)

● **What can you do to overcome that miscommunication? to prevent future misunderstandings?** (I can risk rejection and reach out to my friend; I can admit that I didn't understand; I can try to listen from the other person's perspective.)

THE POINT ▶

Say: **When communication breaks down, relationships suffer. But it doesn't have to be that way. We can learn to spot and avoid common causes of misunderstanding, ▶ and with God's help we can heal the relationships that have been damaged.**

FOR *Even Deeper* DISCUSSION

● Did Jesus want to warn the disciples against everything the Pharisees and Sadducees taught or against something specific? What light might Matthew 16:1-4 shed on Jesus' particular concern?

● Jesus used metaphors and objects from the physical world to teach spiritual lessons. What are the disadvantages of using earthly analogies to teach heavenly truths? What are the advantages?

● What false teachings and values are the "yeast" of today's church? How can we recognize and root out these bad influences?

☐ OPTION 2: *Healing the Hurts*

(15 to 20 minutes)

Direct class members to form pairs. Give each pair a sheet of paper and a pencil. Have each partner write the first names of the five most important people in his or her life on one side of the paper.

After everyone has written the names, say: **It'd be nice if we never had misunderstandings, especially with the really important people in our lives. Unfortunately, it seems that miscommunication and misunderstanding are part of life. However, knowing what causes misunderstandings can help us minimize them. So take several minutes to brainstorm with your partner as many causes of misunderstanding as you can think of. You may want to dis-**

cuss misunderstandings you've had with the people you listed, or you may want to talk about misunderstandings you've observed others having. There's one rule: Each time you name a cause of misunderstanding, tear a fist-sized piece out of the paper. Go.

After several minutes, ask volunteers to name the causes of misunderstanding they identified. Then ask:

- **What was it like to tear up the names of the people most important to you?** (When my partner tore up his names, he tore up mine as well; it was sad to tear up my daughter's name.)
- **How is tearing up names like what misunderstanding does to relationships?** (Misunderstanding tears people out of our lives; we damage our loved ones just as we damaged the paper; our lives end up in pieces.)

Have pairs tape their papers back together, then ask:

- **How well did you mend your paper?** (We taped the pieces back together, but the paper is still damaged; we can read the names again, but it doesn't look very nice.)
- **How is your repaired paper like a repaired relationship? How is it different?** (The tears in both can be mended; neither can be put back together perfectly; a repaired relationship will continue to heal over time.)
- **When it comes to repairing relationships, what can God do that we can't?** (God can turn a bad experience into something good; God can enable us to forgive completely; God can help both partners be objective about what happened.)

Say: **Miscommunication damages relationships, but it doesn't have to destroy them completely. Let's look at God's Word to learn what we can do to heal damaged relationships.**

Have each pair join another to form a foursome. Then assign each group one or more of the following Bible passages:

- **Ecclesiastes 7:8-9**
- **Matthew 18:21-22, 35**
- **Philippians 2:4-5**

Say: **After you read and discuss your passage, answer the following questions.** Ask:

- **What is the principle taught by this passage?**
- **Why should we obey this biblical principle?**
- **What are specific ways we can use this biblical principle to heal a relationship damaged by misunderstanding?**

Allow groups five minutes to read and discuss their passages. Then have each group tell the rest of the class the message of its Bible passage and how it can help heal damaged relationships. During this time, encourage adults to

If you didn't complete the "Misunderstandings" activity, you may want to have groups examine John 3:1-13 at this point. Direct groups to read the passage, then have them discuss the appropriate questions on the "Misunderstandings" handout in their groups.

For the group discussion, consider writing the questions on newsprint so class members can talk at their own pace.

ask clarifying questions if they don't understand what a group means.

After each group has presented its findings, say: **The Bible is filled with helpful advice on how to mend broken relationships, but that advice is useless until we apply it to our own situations. So let's take some time to apply what we've learned. Think of a relationship in which communication is often difficult and sometimes damaging.** Pause. **Now silently answer the following questions.** Allow adults one minute to think about each question. Ask:

- **What makes it difficult for you to communicate with this person? for them to communicate with you?** Pause.
- **What are the frequent causes of miscommunication: differing perspectives? differing styles of communicating? differing levels of commitment? lack of honesty? lack of courage? lack of effort?** Pause.
- **What can you do to overcome the obstacles to communication and minimize the amount of miscommunication? What does the other person need to do?** Pause.
- **What one thing will you do to improve communication the next time you speak with this person?** Pause.

Close the activity in prayer, asking God to give everyone the insight, honesty, courage, and opportunity to heal relationships that have been hurt by miscommunication and misunderstanding.

For *Even Deeper* Discussion

- Matthew 18:21-22 teaches us to forgive others as often as they need it. What does it mean to forgive someone?
- To what extent does forgiveness require us to continue a damaging relationship with someone?
- Is understanding the words that someone speaks the same as understanding the person? Explain. How is believing the facts about Jesus different from believing or trusting Jesus?

The "Apply-It-To-Life This Week" handout (p. 54) helps people further explore the issues uncovered in today's class. Give everyone a photocopy of the handout. Encourage class members to take time during the coming week to explore the questions and activities listed on the handout.

CLOSING

Different Worlds

(up to 10 minutes)

Give each person a sheet of paper and a pencil. Read aloud the following statements and have everyone follow your instructions by drawing the appropriate shapes on their papers.

Say:

- **If you're married, draw a large circle on your paper. If you're currently not married, draw a squiggly line.**
- **Draw a star for each child you have. If you don't have any children, draw a small box.**
- **If you've been baptized, draw a cross somewhere on your paper.**
- **For every move you've made as an adult, draw a wheel on your paper.**
- **Draw a symbol that represents your favorite hobby.**
- **If you've experienced the death of a family member or close friend in the past year, draw a small triangle.**
- **If you've recently changed careers, draw symbols that represent your previous and current careers.**
- **If you've been working at the same job for a long time, draw a symbol of that work and circle it three times.**

Ask for suggestions of other life situations to illustrate. Then have class members compare their drawings with those of the other members of their small groups.

Say: **Each paper is unique, and so is each person here. It can be difficult for people with different backgrounds and experiences to communicate clearly with each other. But with patience, love, and God's guidance, we can avoid misunderstandings. ▶ And when communication does break down, with God's help we can heal our damaged relationships. As we close, think about a relationship that has been damaged by misunderstanding.** Pause. **Now ask God to show you what you can do to heal that relationship.**

◀ THE POINT

Pause. Close in prayer, asking God to give class members the courage to do what they can to heal their damaged relationships.

For Extra Time

THROUGH YOUR EYES
(up to 5 minutes)

One way to increase understanding is to consider the backgrounds and perspectives of our communication partners. Have class members form trios and discuss the challenges to communication that the following people might experience: someone who was sexually abused as a child; someone recently divorced; an only child; someone who can't read well; someone raised in a legalistic church; someone recently fired from a job; a minister; someone who has experienced discrimination; and someone from a different culture. Then ask adults how their own experiences affect the way they communicate and how they can develop relationships with people who have had different experiences.

DISCOVERING PREJUDICES
(up to 5 minutes)

Ask adults to envision the crime as you read the following testimony of a mugging victim.

"I was walking down Maple Street when someone approached me from behind and demanded my valuables. I felt a small, hard object pressed against my back, so I didn't hesitate. I handed back my rings and watch without looking. Then the assailant pushed me to the ground and ran. I heard the sound of running feet, but I didn't move until I was sure the attacker was gone."

Form trios and ask adults to honestly answer the following questions based on their mental depiction of the crime.

- **Did this crime take place in a city or a small town?**
- **Was the victim male or female? young or old?**
- **What was the ethnic background of the victim?**
- **Was the assailant male or female? young or old?**
- **What was the ethnic background of the assailant?**

Then ask:

- **Which answers surprised you most? Explain.**
- **How do prejudices cause communication breakdowns?**
- **How can we keep prejudices from influencing the way we hear things?**

Misunderstandings

MATTHEW 16:5-12

1. **Read Matthew 16:5-12.**
2. **Discuss the questions below.** You have approximately 10 minutes to complete your discussion.
   - What was the misunderstanding in this passage?
   - How did the immediate circumstances cause the disciples to misunderstand Jesus?
   - Read the FYI box at the bottom of the section. Why didn't Jesus warn against the "teaching" of the Pharisees and Sadducees? What did the "yeast" metaphor convey that a literally worded warning could not?
   - What is the connection between the disciples' lack of faith and their failure to understand Jesus' warning (Matthew 16:8, 9, 11)?
   - How did Jesus and the disciples overcome the miscommunication and reach an understanding?
   - What can we learn about the causes and cures of miscommunication from this passage?

FYI It's common for the same metaphorical object to convey different ideas. For example, biblical writers used "yeast" as a metaphor for good (Matthew 13:33; Luke 13:2-21) and for evil (Luke 12:1; 1 Corinthians 5:6-8; Galatians 5:9). The task of the reader is to discover the significance and nuances of the metaphorical object in each case.

JOHN 3:1-13

1. **Read John 3:1-13.**
2. **Discuss the questions below.** You have approximately 10 minutes to complete your discussion.
   - What was the misunderstanding in this passage?
   - Read the FYI box at the bottom of the section. Which meaning of *anōthen* did Jesus intend in John 3:3 and 7? Which meaning did Nicodemus think Jesus intended?
   - With what did Nicodemus associate the terms "born" and "enter" (John 3:4)? With what did Jesus associate them (John 3:3, 5-8)?
   - Why did Nicodemus misunderstand Jesus?
   - What is the connection between Nicodemus' failure to understand Jesus and his refusal to accept or believe Jesus (John 3:10-12)?
   - What can we learn about the causes of miscommunication from this passage?

FYI The Greek word that the New International Version translates "again" in verses 3 and 7 *(anōthen)* also means "from above." In fact, several translations (New Revised Standard Version, Jerusalem Bible) have "from above" in verses 3 and 7, and nearly every English Bible translates *anōthen* as "from above" in John 3:31 and 19:11.

LESSON 3

When Communication Breaks Down

The Point: ▶ With God's help, we can heal relationships that have been hurt by misunderstanding and miscommunication.

Scripture Focus: Matthew 16:5-12 and John 3:1-13

Reflecting on God's Word

Each day this week, read one of the following Scripture passages and think about how you can use it to heal a relationship damaged by miscommunication. Then make a commitment to do what you can to heal that relationship. You may want to list your discoveries and commitments in the space under each passage.

Day 1: Luke 6:31. We should treat others as we want them to treat us.

Day 2: Proverbs 15:1. Words can hurt or heal.

Day 3: Galatians 5:13-15. We serve ourselves best by serving others.

Day 4: John 13:34. We should love others as Christ loved us.

Day 5: Proverbs 24:17. We should take no pleasure in others' misfortune.

Day 6: Matthew 18:21-22. We should forgive others as often as they need it.

Beyond Reflection

1. The most important kind of communication is communication with God. Read Acts 12:5-16 and think about how the believers must have felt when God answered their prayers for Peter's release.

- Have you ever prayed for something without really expecting God to answer your prayer? Why didn't you expect God to respond?
- How has God answered prayers in quick or concrete ways?
- How has God used you to bring an answer to someone else's prayer?

Take a moment to pray now. Ask God to help you know how to pray and how to recognize answers to prayers.

2. Think of a relationship that's recently been hurt by a breakdown in communication. Write a letter to the person involved in that situation and express your feelings and forgiveness (if appropriate). Make a commitment to do all you can to resolve that broken relationship during the coming week.

Next Week's Bible Passage: Acts 26:24-32

Handling Conflict

Skillful communicators can turn unproductive conflict into positive communication.

THE POINT

Objectives

Participants will
- discover how conflict arises out of miscommunication,
- explore several biblical models for dealing with conflict, and
- learn techniques for dealing with conflict in a healthy manner.

Bible Basis

Look up the Scripture. Then read the background paragraphs to see how the passage relates to people today.

ACTS 26:24-32

Acts 26:24-32 tells of Paul's defense before Festus and King Agrippa.

Paul was no stranger to conflict (2 Corinthians 6:3-10), but he knew that sometimes it was best avoided. His appearance before Festus and Agrippa was one of those times. Festus was the new Roman governor of Judea (Acts 24:27). His predecessor, Felix, had kept Paul in prison for two years, hoping either to extract a bribe from Paul or to please the Jewish religious leaders who had accused Paul of defiling the temple (Acts 24:1-9, 24-27).

But now Paul was Festus' problem. Paul had thwarted the Jewish religious leaders' plan to assassinate him by exercising his right as a Roman citizen to appear before the emperor (Acts 25:3, 10-12), but Festus didn't know what to tell Nero about the case.

Herod Agrippa II would help him decide. Agrippa, a

puppet king of the Romans, ruled a small territory to the north of Judea. More important, Agrippa was knowledgeable about Jewish affairs and was in charge of the Jerusalem temple. So when Agrippa and his sister Bernice came to pay their respects to the new governor, Festus asked Agrippa to help specify the charges against Paul.

Paul made the most of his audience before Festus, Agrippa, and Bernice and recounted for them how he had converted from Judaism to become a follower of Christ (Acts 26:2-23). However, he was cut short by Festus when he began to speak of Christ's resurrection. Such talk sounded insane to a sensible Roman such as Festus. Still, Paul was certain that Agrippa did not share Festus' sentiments. Agrippa knew the facts about the life, death, and resurrection of Jesus. Moreover, Agrippa believed the testimony of the prophets, so Paul appealed to him.

Agrippa knew Festus and the others would think he was foolish if he agreed with Paul, so he deflected Paul's question with one of his own. But Paul was not so easily dissuaded. He wanted everyone listening to become what he had become... except, of course, for the chains.

The hearing was over, and everyone agreed that Paul did not deserve death or imprisonment. However, Paul's appeal (and God's plan—see Acts 23:11) had ensured that Paul would go to Rome and appear before an imperial court. There he would continue to defend himself and promote Christ whenever he had the chance to do so.

Paul's conduct before Festus and Agrippa teaches us volumes. Paul didn't dwell on his own innocence and dignity. He ignored Festus' insult and Agrippa's dismissal and sought only to communicate the gospel of Jesus Christ. He was polite, persuasive, and relaxed enough to joke about his chains. Paul knew when conflict was necessary in spreading the gospel and when it was inappropriate and harmful.

It's easy to become angry and defensive when we feel attacked by others. But ranting and raving rarely solve anything. Instead, we can learn from Paul's example that sometimes politeness and a good sense of humor can be more powerful than an angry roar.

We've all been in the uncomfortable position of dealing with conflict caused by miscommunication. Handling conflict in a healthy manner is difficult, yet it's an important skill to develop. This lesson will help adults explore and practice ways to avoid and overcome conflict.

This Lesson at a Glance

Section	*Minutes*	*What Participants Will Do*	*Supplies*
Opening	*up to 10*	**Inflections**—Learn what today's lesson is about and experience how people's inflections can influence communication.	
Bible Exploration and Application	*20 to 30*	☐ *Option 1:* **Conflict Management**—Experience conflict while building houses of cards, then explore how Paul handled conflict in Acts 26:24-32.	Bibles, pencils, paper, "Instructions for Houses of Cards" handouts (p. 59), playing cards
	15 to 20	☐ *Option 2:* **Tough Situations**—Discuss how they'd handle specific conflicts.	"Situations" handouts (p. 64)
Closing	*up to 5*	**Unity**—Pray a unison prayer from Psalm 133.	Bibles
For Extra Time	*up to 5*	**Conflict Resolution in the Bible**—Discover biblical principles for handling conflict.	Bibles
	up to 5	**Course Reflection**—Complete sentences to describe what they've learned from this course.	

OPENING

Inflections

(up to 10 minutes)

As you begin the class, describe what you'll be learning and doing in today's lesson. Use the following statement or your own summary of the main point: **Welcome to the final week of our study on communication. We've been exploring how genuine communication can deepen and strengthen our relationships. Today we're going to examine how ▶ skillful communicators turn unproductive conflict into positive communication.**

Sometimes the way we say something can obscure or change the real meaning of what's being said. Let's try an experiment to see how this works.

Form groups of four. Have each group member think of a polite or neutral sentence to say to the other members of the group. For example, someone might say, "I really like the way this class is going." Instruct adults to use a variety of inflections when they say their sentences. For example, they might speak as though they're angry, confused, bored, or concerned.

After each group member has spoken his or her sentence with at least one inflection, get everyone's attention. In an angry voice, say: **I'm overjoyed that I was able to observe this shameless display of boldness and creativity** (or some other wordy compliment that sounds more like an angry tirade).

Then have groups discuss the following questions. After each question, have volunteers share insights with the whole class. Ask:

- **How did the inflection of your voice affect how your group members heard you?** (I sounded insincere; everyone thought I was angry, but I wasn't; the tone of my voice cancelled out the words I used.)
- **When have you gotten the wrong message because of the *way* something was said to you?** Answers will vary.
- **How can something as simple as a misinterpreted inflection cause conflict in a relationship?** (If you think someone isn't sincere, you may question that person's friendship; you may think someone is bored and doesn't care to talk when he or she is simply tired.)

Say: **Conflict is a regular part of communication with others. ▶ But we can learn how to turn unproductive conflict into positive communication.**

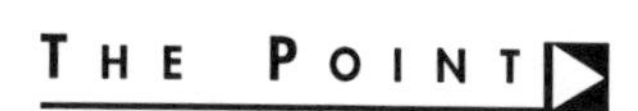

Encourage class members to get involved in the discussions and activities during the study.

Bible Exploration and Application

☐ Option 1: *Conflict Management*

(20 to 30 minutes)

Before class, make enough photocopies of the "Instructions for Houses of Cards" box so that each adult will have one section. Cut apart the sections.

Form groups of four and have adults number off in their groups from one to four. Give each group a deck of playing cards (or a supply of 3×5 cards).

Say: **Many of you probably enjoyed building houses out of cards when you were younger. Well, that's what we're going to do in this activity. But first I'll give each of you instructions that describe how to build your house of cards. Be sure to keep your instructions to yourself.**

Have the ones gather in one corner, the twos in another, and so on. Distribute the appropriate instructions to group members. Then say: **Return to your groups and follow your instructions to build your houses of cards. Oh, yes, and one more thing: No talking.**

Allow several minutes for adults to work on their card houses. It's OK if they guess that each group member has a different agenda. One of this activity's objects is to have people experience being in conflict with one another. When time is up, get everyone's attention and ask:

- **What instructions do you think I gave to the other members of your group?**

After adults call out their guesses, tell adults what you told each group member. Then have adults discuss the following questions one at a time in their original groups. Have the ones answer first, then the twos, and so on. After all group members have answered a question, have volunteers share their groups' insights with the whole class. Ask:

- **How is the way you had slightly different agendas in this activity like the way people relate in real life?** (Conflict may arise when people have different agendas; people don't understand each other because they have different goals.)
- **What did you expect when you began building your house of cards? How did your expectation affect the way you worked?** (I thought we'd all have different ideas, so I waited to see what others would do; I suspected we were given different instructions, but I wanted to build the house my way.)

Instructions for Houses of Cards

Ones: Build the tallest tower that you can.

Twos: Build a tower with as wide a base as possible.

Threes: Build a small, sturdy tower.

Fours: Build an expansive structure with many rooms.

● **How was the conflict in this activity like the conflict you face in daily life? How was it different?** (It was similar because we often don't understand why the conflict came about; it was different because we usually can talk about the conflict.)

● **What are common mistakes people make when attempting to resolve conflict?** (They pretend that nothing is wrong; they become overly defensive; they stop communicating and start fighting; they get sidetracked from the real issues.)

Say: **Just as we had to deal with conflict when we built our houses of cards, we must face conflict in our relationships. But ▶ skillful communicators can turn unproductive conflict into positive communication. Let's look at Acts 26:24-32 to see how Paul did this when he defended his innocence before King Agrippa II and Festus, the Roman governor of Judea.**

THE POINT ▶

BIBLE INSIGHT

Any Roman citizen who feared that a lower court was going to coerce a confession or impose the death sentence could invoke the right of *provocatio ad Caesarem* (appeal to the emperor). This guaranteed the citizen an appearance before an imperial court in Rome. Festus had the legal authority to free an innocent man such as Paul, but it would have been politically unwise for a new governor to exercise such a right.

TEACHER TIP

Be ready to answer the following questions: Who was Festus? What was Paul accused of? Why did Festus think Paul was insane? How did Paul know that King Agrippa believed the prophets? Did King Agrippa mean that Paul had almost convinced him or that he couldn't be convinced in such a short time (Acts 26:28)? Since Festus and Agrippa agreed that Paul was innocent of any wrongdoing, why couldn't they set him free?

As much as possible, have class members answer each other's questions. When necessary, use information from your personal study or this lesson's Bible Basis (pages 55-56) to answer the questions.

Say: **Let's begin by applying active-listening techniques to Acts 26:24-32. Read the passage, paying close attention to what it says and implies. Then compose a one- or two-sentence summary of the passage and list any questions you still have about the passage. In five minutes, we'll report our summaries and answer each other's questions.**

After five minutes, call time and ask groups to report their summaries and questions. After adults have answered each other's questions, ask:

● **How did Paul avoid or minimize conflict?** (He tried to find common ground with Agrippa; he broke the tension by joking about his chains; he didn't take offense at Festus' insult; he appealed to Festus and Agrippa on a personal level.)

● **How did Paul benefit from minimizing conflict?** (Festus and Agrippa formed a favorable opinion of him; Festus probably sent a positive evaluation of his case to Emperor Nero; he maintained a clear conscience.)

Have one member of each group read **Matthew 10:11-16** and another read **Ephesians 4:29-32.**

Say: **Based on these passages and on the way Paul handled conflict in the previous passage you studied, create a list of practical, biblical ways to handle conflict.**

Distribute sheets of paper and pencils so adults can list their ideas. After five minutes, call time and have volunteers share their ideas with the entire class. Then have adults discuss the following questions in their foursomes. Ask:

● **How can you use these principles to minimize**

conflict in one of your relationships? (I can forgive my friend when she hurts me; I can stop criticizing my supervisor in front of my co-workers; I can walk away when someone makes me angry.)

● **What do you think will happen if you practice these principles on a regular basis?** (My friend will feel accepted by me; I'll create a healthy work environment; I'll be able to confront others in love rather than in anger.)

Say: **As we can see from these ideas, the Bible is filled with good advice on dealing with others. As we apply that advice to our lives, we can become ▶ skillful communicators who turn unproductive conflict into positive communication.**

◀ THE POINT

FOR *Even Deeper* DISCUSSION

● Sometimes Jesus provoked conflict (Mark 11:15-19); other times he advocated avoiding it at all costs (Matthew 5:38-42). How do we know when to avoid conflict? when to provoke it?

● What does Jesus mean when he tells the disciples that he is sending them out "like sheep among wolves"? What does it mean to be "as shrewd as snakes and as innocent as doves" (Matthew 10:16)? (If necessary, review the principles for interpreting metaphors on p. 47).

● Jesus told his disciples in Matthew 10:14 to walk away from people who rejected their message. Should we give up on people who reject us?

BIBLE INSIGHT

Matthew 10:11-16 records a part of the instructions Jesus gave to his disciples when he sent them out to minister and preach (see Matthew 10:1-42; Mark 6:6b-12; Luke 9:1-6; 10:1-16). Since the disciples were as helpless as sheep surrounded by a pack of wolves, they needed to be prudent enough to avoid needless conflict but not so suspicious that they became paranoid and isolated.

☐ OPTION 2: *Tough Situations*

(15 to 20 minutes)

Before class, make enough copies of the "Situations" handout (p. 64) so that each foursome may have one.

Give a photocopy of the "Situations" handout to each group. Say: **Choose two of the situations on the handout and practice handling the situations using the biblical concepts we've discussed today. Involve each person in your group as either an actor or an advisor.**

Remind adults that role-playing these scenarios will prepare them to handle similar situations in everyday life. Encourage adults to "get into" their characters and to

TEACHER TIP

If you did not complete the "Conflict Management" activity, form groups of four. Then assign Acts 26:24-32 to one-half of the groups and Ephesians 4:29-32 to the other half. Tell groups to list all of the ways their passages can help them avoid unnecessary conflict. After several minutes, ask groups to report their findings.

TEACHER
TIP

Some class members may be uncomfortable with role-playing, but the rewards of role-playing far outweigh its risks. Encourage class members to loosen up and learn through this active learning technique.

interact in the improvised conflict situations.

After about 10 minutes, call adults together. Have volunteers share with the whole group what they learned from their role-plays or discussions. Then ask:

- **Which of the situations do you identify with most closely?** Answers will vary.
- **What can you do to overcome conflict in your situation?** (My spouse and I can agree on and always use a compromise method of discipline; I can involve those with more job experience in the decision-making process; I can emphasize areas of agreement rather than disagreement.)
- **What biblical principles should we remember when we face conflict?** (Our pride is not as important as genuine communication; sometimes it's best simply to walk away; humor can defuse a tense situation; we need to find common ground with our conversation partners.)

THE POINT ▶

Say: **Paul knew how to avoid conflict in a potentially deadly situation. As we learn from his and other biblical examples, ▶ we can become the kind of skillful communicators who turn unproductive conflict into positive communication. Let's commit to using these insights when we encounter the inevitable misunderstandings that come with relationships.**

FOR *Even Deeper* DISCUSSION

- According to Acts 25:9-12, Paul rejected Festus' suggestion of a trial in Jerusalem and claimed his right as a Roman citizen to have his case heard before the emperor. When should we claim our rights? When should we give up our rights to avoid conflict?
- Ephesians 4:29 teaches that we should speak only that which builds others up. To what extent may this include accusing others of sin or warning them of divine judgment? How should Paul's command affect the manner in which we accuse or warn?

APPLY-IT-TO LIFE THIS WEEK

The "Apply-It-To-Life This Week" handout (p. 65) helps people further explore the issues uncovered in today's class. Give everyone a photocopy of the handout. Encourage class members to take time during the coming week to explore the questions and activities listed on the handout.

CLOSING

Unity

(up to 5 minutes)

Form a circle. Make sure everyone has access to the same Bible translation. Say: **Psalm 133 sings the praises of people who are unified. As we close our series on communication, let's thank God together for the wisdom we've been granted through each person's contributions to the class. We'll read Psalm 133 together as our song of unity, then I'll close in prayer.**

After reading Psalm 133 aloud, close with a prayer similar to the following: **Dear God, thank you for the relationships in our lives. ▶ Help us to become skillful communicators who turn unproductive conflict into positive communication. Teach us to be the best communicators we can be. Amen.**

Ask adults what they liked most about the course and what they'd like to see different about it. Please note their comments (along with your own) and send them to the Adult Curriculum Editor at Group Publishing, Dept. BK, Box 481, Loveland, CO 80539. We want your feedback so we can make each course we publish better than the last. Thanks!

For Extra Time

CONFLICT RESOLUTION IN THE BIBLE

(up to 5 minutes)

Form groups of no more than five. Assign one of the following passages to each group: Genesis 13:1-18; Amos 7:10-17; Acts 15:1-11. Instruct groups to read their passages and discuss how well the conflict situations were handled in terms of the biblical principles listed earlier. If you prefer, have groups look up the following verses in Proverbs to discover additional principles for avoiding and overcoming conflict: 10:19; 15:1; 17:9, 14; 18:13; 24:26; 26:4-5, 17; 29:20.

COURSE REFLECTION

(up to 5 minutes)

Ask class members to reflect on the past four lessons. Then have them take turns completing the following sentences:

- Something I learned in this course was...
- If I could tell friends about this course, I'd say...
- Something I'll do differently because of this course is...

Situations

Choose two of the situations listed below to role play in your group. Group members who aren't playing a role should observe and suggest ways to deal with the conflict.

Situation One: Blaming

Issue: Two friends in a car have just driven into a ditch. The front of the car was damaged in the accident, so the car can't be driven.
Ted, the owner and driver of the car, blames Bill, a passenger, for being a distraction and causing the accident.
Bill claims that Ted wasn't paying attention to the road and is responsible for the accident. Bill suffered a minor cut on his forehead during the accident.

Situation Two: Power Struggle

Issue: A new supervisor wants to change well-established job responsibilities.
Janet is a young supervisor who wants everyone on the construction crew to rotate among the various jobs.
Ron is an employee with 15 years of experience. Ron thinks that the new policy is unfair to those with seniority and will prove to be less efficient than the old policy.

Situation Three: Theological Disagreement

Issue: Two members of a church disagree on the correct interpretation of the book of Revelation.
Sandra believes that Revelation is a prophetic message describing specific events and that it's predicting the return of Christ in the near future.
Mary believes that Revelation is a historical account of events that have already taken place. It's significant not for its specific predictions but only because it teaches that "Christians will win in the end."

Situation Four: Home Fires

Issue: A husband and wife disagree on the proper method of disciplining their children.
Tom believes that children require strict, sometimes physical, discipline. Tom feels undermined by Donna's rejection of corporal punishment.
Donna believes that corporal punishment demeans kids and refuses to use it. Donna thinks that kids should learn by experiencing the consequences of their choices.

LESSON 4

Handling Conflict

The Point: ▶ Skillful communicators can turn unproductive conflict into positive communication.

Scripture Focus: Acts 26:24-32

Reflecting on God's Word

Each day this week, read one of the following Scripture passages and examine the conflicts described. Condsider what caused the conflict, what steps were taken toward resolving the conflict, and what the conflict's outcome was. You may want to record your discoveries in the space under each passage.

Day 1: Genesis 13:1-18. Abram and Lot part ways.

Day 2: 1 Samuel 24:1-22. David allows Saul to live.

Day 3: 1 Kings 12:1-24. Israel rebels against Rehoboam.

Day 4: Amos 7:10-17. Amaziah orders Amos to stop prophesying.

Day 5: Acts 4:1-31. Peter and John testify before the Sanhedrin.

Day 6: Acts 15:1-11. The Jerusalem church accepts Gentile converts.

Beyond Reflection

1. Begin by keeping a journal of your conflicts and how you deal with them. After a couple of weeks, read your journal entries and compare your methods of dealing with conflict with those you studied in class.

2. Watch a few popular TV shows and examine how the characters deal with conflict.

- What causes the most conflict in these TV shows?
- What are good ways the characters deal with conflict? bad ways?
- How would the characters be different if they followed the biblical principles for handling conflict?

Fellowship and Outreach Specials

Use the following activities any time you want. You can use them as part of (or in place of) your regular class activities, or you can plan a special event based on one or more of the ideas.

Difficult Communication

Have each adult choose someone to talk with who comes from a very different background. Ask each class member to engage that person in conversation about some aspect of his or her life that's foreign to the class member. For example, adults could ask their partners what it's like to be a student in the 1990s, what it's like being married or single, or what it's like to recover from drug or alcohol addiction.

Meet later with class members to discuss the communication experience. Ask:

- **What did you hear the person saying that you'd never heard before?**
- **What did you appreciate most about the person you talked with?**
- **How has your perspective widened? What did you learn about yourself from this communication experience?**
- **How is reaching out to people you don't usually speak with like what Jesus did in his ministry?**

Encourage adults to widen their worlds by spending time talking with people they don't normally speak with.

Who's on First?

Get a copy of the classic comedy bit "Who's on First?" made famous by Abbott and Costello. Have adults discuss how this funny display of miscommunication is like or unlike what happens in real life. For fun, have class members create their own skits on miscommunication. Have them perform these skits for each other then discuss their implications.

Something to Share

The most important thing we can communicate to others is our faith. Have class members create fliers listing the programs and worship times at your church. Also include quotes about how the church has been helpful to your adults. Then have everyone distribute the fliers in the community and offer warm invitations for church neighbors to visit your church.

This Call's for You

One of the greatest things we can communicate to others is gratitude for what they've done to serve us. Have class members prepare a list of people who've volunteered to help at church or in the local community. Divide the list among small groups and have groups call the people to thank them for serving. You might see if you can meet at a local business that has multiple open phone lines so you can do this activity together.

Actions Speak Louder

Volunteer as a group to help at a local organization that feeds, clothes, or otherwise provides for people. Your presence and helping hands say more to people than any words you can offer. Afterward, meet briefly to discuss the experience.

Hymn Sing and Potluck

Invite your entire congregation to a hymn sing and potluck dinner sponsored by your class. During the event, examine the hymns to see how clearly their words express the Christian faith for each of the generational groups at the event. Have adults, teenagers, and children choose the hymns or songs that best express their faith. Then, in your church services, use what you've learned at the hymn sing to meet the needs of all age groups when singing hymns and songs.

Read My Recipe

Plan a dinner for just your class or include adults and children of all ages. Provide some of the attendees with recipes for creating part of the meal. Have these people sit at tables and give verbal instructions to the other adults and children for cooking or preparing the menu items. For example, someone with a recipe for salad would read the recipe aloud, step by step, so that another person or group of people could create the salad, using the supplies in the kitchen. In order to complete the salad according to the recipe, the preparers would need to communicate regularly with the recipe holder. Talk about the importance of clear communication in this activity. Serve the meal and talk about the role communication played in getting the food to the table.

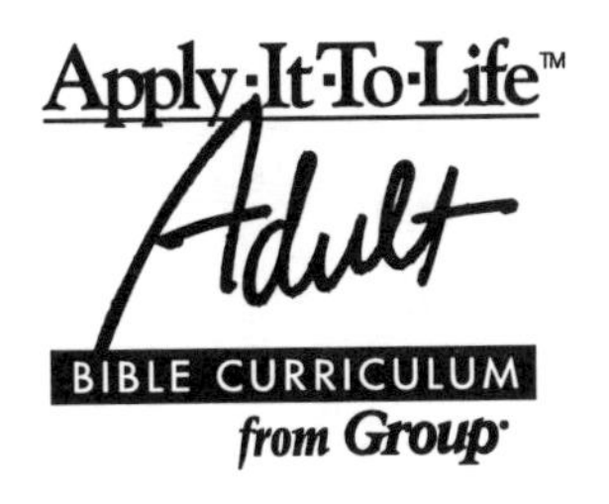
Apply-It-To-Life™
Adult
BIBLE CURRICULUM
from Group

Notes